Verbal Reasoning: Sequences, Logic & Coding

The 11+ 10-Minute Tests

For GL & other test providers

Ages
10-11

Practise • Prepare • Pass
Everything your child needs for 11+ success

How to use this book

This book is made up of 10-minute tests and puzzle pages.
There are answers and detailed explanations in the pull-out section at the back of the book.

10-Minute Tests

- There are 37 tests in this book, each containing either 14 or 16 questions. These tests provide bite-sized practice for specific skills tested in the full-length 11+ test.

- Each test is targeted to cover a range of sequence, logic and coding question styles that your child could come across in their 11+ test, at the same difficulty level.

- Your child should aim to score at least 12 out of 14 or 14 out of 16 in each 10-minute test. If they score less than this, use their results to work out the areas they need more practice on.

- If your child hasn't managed to finish the test in time, they need to work on increasing their speed, whereas if they have made a lot of mistakes, they need to work more carefully.

- Keep track of your child's scores using the progress chart on the inside back cover of the book.

Puzzle Pages

- There are 10 puzzle pages in this book, which are a great break from test-style questions. They encourage children to practise the same skills that they will need in the test, but in a fun way.

Published by CGP

Editors:
Marc Barnard, Heather Cowley, Zoe Fenwick, Andy Park

With thanks to Chloe Anderson and Judith Hornigold for the proofreading.

ISBN: 978 1 78294 938 1
Printed by Elanders Ltd, Newcastle upon Tyne
Clipart from Corel®

Based on the classic CGP style created by Richard Parsons.

Contents

Test 1

You have **10 minutes** to do this test. Work as quickly and accurately as you can.

Find the missing number to complete each sum. Write your answer on the line.

Example: 7 + 5 = 24 ÷ (___2___)

1. 11 + 20 = 42 – (________)

2. 2 × 7 + 11 = 20 + (________)

3. 9 × 3 + 5 = 37 – (________)

4. 20 – 13 = 8 ÷ (________) + 3

Underline the pair of letters that completes each sentence in the most sensible way. Use the alphabet to help you.

A B C D E F G H I J K L M N O P Q R S T U V W X Y Z

Example: **DG** is to **FE** as **RU** is to (<u>TS</u> SR TU ST US).

5. **HF** is to **FN** as **NO** is to (LX LW NW KX OW).

6. **RC** is to **LB** as **ZL** is to (TK TN WM TL TH).

7. **KS** is to **QP** as **EU** is to (NS LU MR KQ KR).

8. **GE** is to **KA** as **LN** is to (RM OJ PH PM PJ).

Find the pair of letters that continues each sequence in the best way. Use the alphabet to help you.

A B C D E F G H I J K L M N O P Q R S T U V W X Y Z

Example: TU QR NO KL HI (EF)

9. TY WA ZC CE FG (______)

10. SD VE YI BJ EN (______)

11. AH WM SQ OT KV (______)

12. PT QV UY VC ZH (______)

Find the number that completes the final set of numbers in the same way as the first two sets. Write your answer on the line.

Example: 7 (4) 3 10 (5) 5 15 (11) 4

13. 16 (2) 8 36 (4) 9 6 (______) 2

14. 4 (8) 1 3 (18) 3 5 (______) 4

15. 9 (24) 3 6 (32) 10 6 (______) 9

16. 12 (7) 3 6 (5) 2 8 (______) 2

END OF TEST

/ 16

Test 2

You have **10 minutes** to do this test. Work as quickly and accurately as you can.

Find the number that continues each sequence in the best way. Write your answer on the line.

Example: 3 6 9 12 15 (18)

1. 4 12 20 28 36 (______)
2. 42 47 39 43 36 39 (______)
3. 36 33 29 24 18 (______)
4. 31 29 33 28 35 27 (______)

Each question uses a different code. Use the alphabet to help you work out the answer to each question.

A B C D E F G H I J K L M N O P Q R S T U V W X Y Z

Example: If the code for **MANY** is **LZMX**, what is the code for **GREY**? (FQDX)

5. If the code for **LEAF** is **KDZE**, what is the code for **WORD**? (____________)
6. If the code for **LICK** is **JKAM**, what is **NQJQ** the code for? (____________)
7. If the code for **FILM** is **URON**, what is **SZMW** the code for? (____________)
8. If the code for **BILL** is **AGIH**, what is the code for **PORK**? (____________)

Each letter stands for a number. Work out the answer to each sum as a letter. Write your answer on the line.

Example: A = 1 B = 2 C = 6 D = 12 E = 10 D ÷ B = (C)

9. A = 1 B = 3 C = 5 D = 6 E = 7 B + C – A = (________)

10. A = 2 B = 3 C = 4 D = 6 E = 22 B × D + C = (________)

11. A = 6 B = 9 C = 10 D = 11 E = 50 E ÷ C + A = (________)

12. A = 7 B = 5 C = 12 D = 15 E = 42 E ÷ A × B + C = (________)

Read the information carefully, then use it to answer the question that follows.

13. Mavis, Caitlin, Faisal, Pierrick and Eleanor are making pizzas. They have four toppings to choose from: chicken, pepperoni, mushrooms and sweetcorn. Mavis puts sweetcorn and pepperoni on her pizza. Faisal has chicken, mushrooms and pepperoni. Eleanor is vegetarian. Pierrick has pepperoni and mushrooms. Caitlin hates mushrooms, but she has more toppings than Pierrick.

If the statements above are true, only one of the sentences below **must** be true. Which one? Circle the correct letter.

A Mavis's pizza has fewer toppings than Caitlin's.

B Eleanor's pizza has the fewest toppings.

C Caitlin has as many toppings as Pierrick.

D Faisal has fewer toppings than Eleanor.

E Eleanor has sweetcorn on her pizza.

14. Marc, Ellen, Nasreen, Saif and Rosa are travelling to Birmingham. Rosa arrives before Nasreen. Marc arrives 20 minutes after Rosa. Saif arrives half an hour after Nasreen. Ellen arrives last.

If the statements above are true, only one of the sentences below **must** be true. Which one? Circle the correct letter.

A Marc and Rosa arrive before Nasreen.

B Nasreen arrives second.

C Ellen arrives at the same time as Rosa.

D Rosa arrives 20 minutes after Marc.

E Saif arrives second to last.

END OF TEST

/ 14

Puzzles 1

This is a good time for a break. Practise your **maths** and **sequences** skills below.

Hideaway House

The secret meeting place of the Dazzle Detectives has been discovered. Amy Cluesolver has left a note to tell her fellow detectives the new location.

The number code starts on **1**. It follows the sequence **+6**, **-2**.
Shade the numbers in the sequence on the grid below.
Then read across the shaded letters to find the location.

1	2	3	4	5	6	7	8	9	10
S	F	G	L	N	B	E	V	A	M

11	12	13	14	15	16	17	18	19	20
K	H	E	D	R	J	T	Q	O	I

21	22	23	24	25	26	27	28	29	30
N	P	W	Z	A	H	Y	U	X	C

The location of the new hideout is:

_ _ _ _ _ _ _ _ _ _ _   _ _ _

Sneaky Sums

Some of the numbers in the sums below have been replaced with shapes.
Each shape stands for the same number every time.
Look for patterns in the sums and write the missing number inside each shape.

○ × ○ = 9   ⬡ × 2 = □   ⬡ + ○ = □ − ○

□ + ⬡ + ⬡ − ○ = 21

Test 3

You have **10 minutes** to do this test. Work as quickly and accurately as you can.

The number codes for three of these four words are listed in a random order. Work out the code to answer the questions.

BOAT **BATS** **SNOB** **ANTS**

1324 **4265** **6351**

1. Find the code for the word **BATS**. (________)

2. Find the code for the word **TONS**. (________)

3. Find the word that has the number code **1564**. (________)

Find the pair of letters that continues each sequence in the best way. Use the alphabet to help you.

A B C D E F G H I J K L M N O P Q R S T U V W X Y Z

Example: TU QR NO KL HI (EF)

4. EH CI AJ YK WL (______)

5. BI DJ GF IG LC (______)

6. RJ MH HE CA XV (______)

7. TM XK AI EG HE (______)

Find the missing number to complete each sum. Write your answer on the line.

Example: 7 + 5 = 24 ÷ (2)

8. 18 + 17 = 37 – (________)

9. 35 ÷ 7 + 14 = 12 + (________)

10. 27 ÷ 3 + 9 = 10 + (________)

11. 36 ÷ 9 + 14 = 2 × (________)

12. 17 – 9 = 5 + (________) – 1

Underline the pair of letters that completes each sentence in the most sensible way. Use the alphabet to help you.

A B C D E F G H I J K L M N O P Q R S T U V W X Y Z

Example: **DG** is to **FE** as **RU** is to (TS SR TU ST US).

13. **KX** is to **MT** as **IU** is to (KN HJ HM KQ KO).

14. **DT** is to **GW** as **AI** is to (DL DK CL DF CF).

15. **AB** is to **BJ** as **LD** is to (LN OL MI ML MJ).

16. **WZ** is to **DA** as **VD** is to (FY EV EW CU CW).

END OF TEST

/ 16

Test 4

10

You have **10 minutes** to do this test. Work as quickly and accurately as you can.

Find the number that completes the final set of numbers in the same way as the first two sets. Write your answer on the line.

Example: 7 (4) 3   10 (5) 5   15 (11) 4

1. 25 (5) 5   24 (4) 6   70 (______) 7
2. 3 (8) 1   10 (21) 7   4 (______) 1
3. 9 (4) 4   6 (2) 3   9 (______) 5
4. 8 (4) 4   6 (5) 9   5 (______) 4

The number codes for three of these four words are listed in a random order. Work out the code to answer the questions.

GIFT   GOLF   FLIT   TOIL

2164   4513   2536

5. Find the code for the word **GOLF**. (__________)
6. Find the code for the word **GILT**. (__________)
7. Find the word that has the number code **3564**. (__________)

Each letter stands for a number. Work out the answer to each sum as a letter. Write your answer on the line.

Example: A = 1 B = 2 C = 6 D = 12 E = 10 D ÷ B = (C)

8. A = 2 B = 3 C = 4 D = 9 E = 14 C × B + A = (______)

9. A = 1 B = 4 C = 9 D = 11 E = 40 E ÷ B + A = (______)

10. A = 2 B = 6 C = 7 D = 15 E = 23 A × C + D – B = (______)

11. A = 3 B = 8 C = 9 D = 12 E = 24 E ÷ B + C – A = (______)

Find the pair of letters that continues each sequence in the best way. Use the alphabet to help you.

A B C D E F G H I J K L M N O P Q R S T U V W X Y Z

Example: TU QR NO KL HI (EF)

12. BN ZI XD VY TT (______)

13. LB MG NM OT PB (______)

14. YR AQ EP GO KN (______)

15. RO PP US SX XE (______)

16. KR PS VN CO KJ (______)

END OF TEST

/ 16

Test 5

You have **10 minutes** to do this test. Work as quickly and accurately as you can.

Each letter stands for a number. Work out the answer to each sum as a letter. Write your answer on the line.

Example: A = 1 B = 2 C = 6 D = 12 E = 10 D ÷ B = (C)

1. A = 2 B = 5 C = 6 D = 10 E = 15 D × A – B = (________)

2. A = 5 B = 7 C = 8 D = 10 E = 12 B + D – E = (________)

3. A = 1 B = 2 C = 7 D = 10 E = 11 A + E – D = (________)

4. A = 2 B = 8 C = 15 D = 17 E = 18 E ÷ A + B – C = (________)

Read the information carefully, then use it to answer the question that follows.

5. Gregory, Leonard, Amélie, Helena and Sid were playing catch. Leonard passed the ball to Amélie. Amélie only had the ball once. Gregory was the only person to never have the ball. Sid was second to have the ball. No-one passed the ball to Helena.

   If the statements above are true, only one of the sentences below **must** be true. Which one? Circle the correct letter.

   A Leonard passed the ball to Helena.
   B Gregory had the ball at the end of the game.
   C Helena had the ball at the start of the game.
   D Sid passed the ball to Amélie.
   E Leonard passed the ball to Sid.

6. Johnny has made too many plans for Saturday. He said he would go bowling with Cathy for an hour at 2 o'clock. He is planning to go ice skating with Miriam before they go for dinner at six. He wants to play rugby with Naseem for an hour and a half, starting two hours before his film with Natalie begins. Lewis is expecting Johnny to go shopping with him at 3 o'clock. This will take double the time as his rugby practice. He wants to go to the cinema with Natalie an hour after he said he would start bowling with Cathy. The film lasts an hour and a half.

If the statements above are true, only one of the sentences below **cannot** be true. Which one? Circle the correct letter.

A Johnny has time to do three different activities.

B He plans to spend twice as long with Miriam as he does with Cathy.

C He has time to go play rugby with Naseem and go shopping with Lewis.

D He can go shopping with Lewis and for dinner with Miriam.

E No other plans overlap with his plans with Miriam.

Find the number that continues each sequence in the best way. Write your answer on the line.

Example: 3 6 9 12 15 (18)

7.	96	48	24	12	6		(______)
8.	3	6	11	18	27		(______)
9.	74	73	73	74	76		(______)
10.	88	8	44	16	22	32	(______)

Each question uses a different code. Use the alphabet to help you work out the answer to each question.

A B C D E F G H I J K L M N O P Q R S T U V W X Y Z

Example: If the code for **MANY** is **LZMX**, what is the code for **GREY**? (FQDX)

11. If the code for **LUCK** is **IRZH**, what is the code for **BEAN**? (__________)

12. If the code for **FETA** is **GDUZ**, what is the code for **LESS**? (__________)

13. If the code for **AREA** is **EUID**, what is **ALPW** the code for? (__________)

14. If the code for **POEM** is **RRIR**, what is **THEW** the code for? (__________)

END OF TEST

/ 14

Test 6

You have **10 minutes** to do this test. Work as quickly and accurately as you can.

Each question uses a different code. Use the alphabet to help you work out the answer to each question.

A B C D E F G H I J K L M N O P Q R S T U V W X Y Z

Example: If the code for **MANY** is **LZMX**, what is the code for **GREY**? (FQDX)

1. If the code for **PINK** is **TMRO**, what is the code for **OWLS**? (________)
2. If the code for **DEAL** is **EGBN**, what is **WGOF** the code for? (________)
3. If the code for **QUAY** is **USEW**, what is **XYBG** the code for? (________)
4. If the code for **MONK** is **KOPO**, what is the code for **OVAL**? (________)

Find the missing number to complete each sum. Write your answer on the line.

Example: 7 + 5 = 24 ÷ (2)

5. 110 ÷ 11 = 16 – (________)
6. 9 × 10 + 5 = 91 + (________)
7. 32 ÷ 4 + 13 = 3 × (________)
8. 8 × 6 – 3 = 9 × (________)

Underline the pair of letters that completes each sentence in the most sensible way. Use the alphabet to help you.

A B C D E F G H I J K L M N O P Q R S T U V W X Y Z

Example: **DG** is to **FE** as **RU** is to (TS SR TU ST US).

9. **QE** is to **UD** as **LC** is to (NZ RB RY PB PC).

10. **IW** is to **DO** as **SN** is to (PF NF NH ME QD).

11. **ME** is to **KK** as **SQ** is to (NT QW NY QU QX).

12. **PS** is to **KH** as **NE** is to (MX MW KX LU MV).

Find the number that continues each sequence in the best way. Write your answer on the line.

Example: 3 6 9 12 15 (18)

13. 46 39 32 25 18 (______)

14. 26 28 32 38 46 (______)

15. 30 17 24 18 18 19 (______)

16. 1 5 13 25 41 (______)

END OF TEST

/ 16

Puzzles 2

Puzzle time! These are a great way to practise your **riddle-solving** and **sequence** skills.

Biscuit Thief

Super sleuth Sally Sandwich is trying to get to the bottom of who ate all her biscuits. She has five suspects: her brother, Gaz, and four friends. She has collected some witness statements, but she knows one person is lying.

Vera — *"There was a trail of crumbs going towards Gaz's room. I was with Parvati!"*

Tommy — *"I was helping my mum hang the washing out."*

Gaz — *"I was playing video games with Si."*

Parvati — *"I saw a boy going into Gaz's room. I'm not sure who it was."*

Si — *"Me and Gaz had to go inside. It was too wet to play football."*

Who do you think stole the biscuits? ____________

Train Timetable

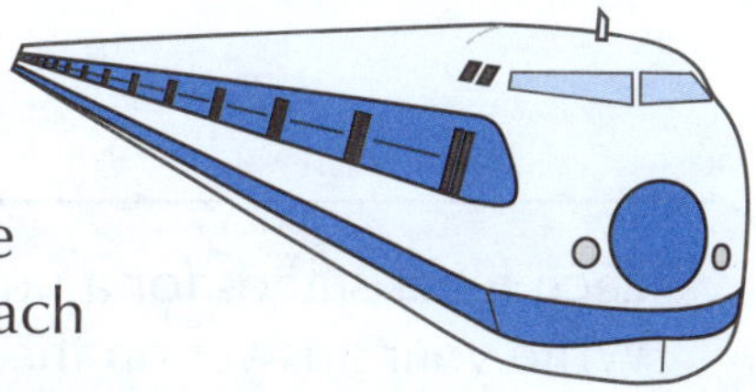

Keshia lives in Benthwaite and wants to know when some trains will pass through her town. Each service travels at a different speed. Look at the patterns in the train times below to find out when each train gets to Benthwaite.

Service name	Bumblebury	Fendon-on-Sea	Headley Grove	Wallington Central	Breckham Parkway	Benthwaite
Wallington Wizard	11:10	11:17	11:24	11:31	11:38	
Parkway Panther	11:45	11:54	12:03	12:12	12:21	
Benthwaite Slug	12:08	12:13	12:19	12:26	12:34	
Bumblebury Crawler	12:21	12:25	12:31	12:39	12:49	
Headley Hopper	12:49	12:52	12:58	13:07	13:19	

Test 7

You have **10 minutes** to do this test. Work as quickly and accurately as you can.

Find the pair of letters that continues each sequence in the best way. Use the alphabet to help you.

A B C D E F G H I J K L M N O P Q R S T U V W X Y Z

Example: TU QR NO KL HI (EF)

1. JO FN BM XL TK (______)
2. JK EH ZD UY PS (______)
3. KQ LN QK RH WE (______)
4. OK PM SQ XS EW (______)
5. PW NB MF KI JK (______)

Each letter stands for a number. Work out the answer to each sum as a letter. Write your answer on the line.

Example: A = 1 B = 2 C = 6 D = 12 E = 10 D ÷ B = (C)

6. A = 1 B = 3 C = 8 D = 9 E = 10 B + C – A = (______)
7. A = 1 B = 3 C = 5 D = 15 E = 20 A × B × C = (______)
8. A = 2 B = 5 C = 7 D = 8 E = 15 E ÷ B + C – D = (______)
9. A = 1 B = 2 C = 9 D = 17 E = 19 B × C + A – D = (______)

Read the information carefully, then use it to answer the question that follows.

10. Gráinne, Tim, Louise, Waqar and Keith have been selling cakes to raise money for charity. Louise raised twice as much as Gráinne. Tim raised £80. The smallest amount raised was £25. Waqar raised twice as much as Keith. Keith did not raise the smallest amount.

If the statements above are true, only one of the sentences below **must** be true. Which one? Circle the correct letter.

A Tim raised more than Waqar.

B Keith raised twice as much as Louise.

C Gráinne raised the smallest amount.

D The largest amount raised was £80.

E Louise raised £70.

11. Tasha, Perrie, Kay, Avi and Raj are talking about their families. Everybody but Perrie has at least 1 brother. Tasha and Avi have more brothers than Kay and Raj. Raj and Avi have 2 sisters. Avi has more siblings than Perrie has cousins. Kay has 1 sister. Tasha has 2 siblings in total. Perrie is an only child, but she has 4 cousins.

If the statements above are true, only one of the sentences below **cannot** be true. Which one? Circle the correct letter.

A Tasha has 2 brothers.

B Avi has 5 siblings.

C Tasha has a brother and a sister.

D Avi has more brothers than Tasha.

E Kay has 2 siblings.

The number codes for three of these four words are listed in a random order.
Work out the code to answer the questions.

EARL TRAM LATE MELT
3456 6423 5241

12. Find the code for the word **MELT**. (________)

13. Find the code for the word **MALE**. (________)

14. Find the word that has the number code **2456**. (________)

END OF TEST

/ 14

Test 8

10

You have **10 minutes** to do this test. Work as quickly and accurately as you can.

Find the number that completes the final set of numbers in the same way as the first two sets. Write your answer on the line.

Example: 7 (4) 3 10 (5) 5 15 (11) 4

1. 2 (9) 6 3 (8) 4 9 (______) 4

2. 7 (5) 3 12 (16) 20 15 (______) 9

3. 4 (6) 5 10 (9) 2 8 (______) 5

4. 40 (10) 8 16 (9) 4 18 (______) 6

Find the pair of letters that continues each sequence in the best way. Use the alphabet to help you.

A B C D E F G H I J K L M N O P Q R S T U V W X Y Z

Example: TU QR NO KL HI (EF)

5. QR RP SN TL UJ (______)

6. OE QA SW US WO (______)

7. LQ HV DZ ZC VE (______)

8. ZU AS CT FR JS (______)

Each letter stands for a number. Work out the answer to each sum as a letter.
Write your answer on the line.

Example: A = 1 B = 2 C = 6 D = 12 E = 10 D ÷ B = (C)

9. A = 1 B = 8 C = 11 D = 18 E = 14 B + C – A = (________)

10. A = 1 B = 8 C = 10 D = 11 E = 13 C + D – B = (________)

11. A = 2 B = 10 C = 14 D = 24 E = 50 E ÷ B × A = (________)

12. A = 5 B = 6 C = 7 D = 30 E = 35 D ÷ B × C – A = (________)

Read the information carefully, then use it to answer the question that follows.

13. Katrina, Nigella, Tristan, Dania and Stuart are growing sunflowers at school. Nigella's sunflower is 40cm taller than Stuart's. Tristan's sunflower is the only one to not grow over one metre tall. Dania's sunflower is 2.2m tall. Stuart's sunflower is double the height of Tristan's. Katrina's sunflower is the second tallest.

If the statements above are true, only one of the sentences below **must** be true. Which one? Circle the correct letter.

A Dania grew the tallest sunflower.

B Katrina's sunflower was taller than Dania's.

C Nigella's sunflower was 1.4m taller than Tristan's.

D Stuart's sunflower was the second smallest.

E Katrina's sunflower was 2m tall.

14. Rohan is a waiter. He takes an order for a group of 26 people. At least 1 person orders fish and chips, the least popular dish. 6 people order pizza, which is twice the number of people who order bangers and mash. 4 people order lasagne. Everyone else in the group ordered steak.

If the statements above are true, only one of the sentences below **cannot** be true. Which one? Circle the correct letter.

A More people ordered pizza than lasagne.

B Bangers and mash was the second least popular dish.

C More people ordered bangers and mash than fish and chips.

D A total of 10 people ordered steak.

E More people ordered pizza than those who ordered bangers and mash and fish and chips put together.

END OF TEST

/ 14

Test 9

You have **10 minutes** to do this test. Work as quickly and accurately as you can.

Underline the pair of letters that completes each sentence in the most sensible way. Use the alphabet to help you.

A B C D E F G H I J K L M N O P Q R S T U V W X Y Z

Example: **DG** is to **FE** as **RU** is to (TS SR TU ST US).

1. **SQ** is to **KS** as **RT** is to (IV JV JS IT IU).
2. **LN** is to **OT** as **AJ** is to (DQ DM DP AR DR).
3. **HR** is to **CZ** as **WB** is to (UK RH OJ QJ RJ).
4. **MU** is to **GV** as **RG** is to (OK OF LH LK LJ).

Find the number that continues each sequence in the best way. Write your answer on the line.

Example: 3 6 9 12 15 (18)

5. 3 6 12 24 (____)
6. 50 40 46 35 42 30 (____)
7. 5 8 13 20 29 40 (____)
8. 51 56 60 63 65 (____)

Find the missing number to complete each sum. Write your answer on the line.

Example: 7 + 5 = 24 ÷ (2)

9. 37 – 10 = 3 × (________)

10. 9 × 6 + 5 = 70 – (________)

11. 3 × 4 + 12 = 8 × (________)

12. 70 ÷ 10 + 15 = 6 × (________) – 2

Each question uses a different code. Use the alphabet to help you work out the answer to each question.

A B C D E F G H I J K L M N O P Q R S T U V W X Y Z

Example: If the code for **MANY** is **LZMX**, what is the code for **GREY**? (FQDX)

13. If the code for **DUAL** is **ZQWH**, what is the code for **ZERO**? (________)

14. If the code for **PERK** is **QISO**, what is **CYAD** the code for? (________)

15. If the code for **BULK** is **YFOP**, what is **ORNK** the code for? (________)

16. If the code for **WRIT** is **ZTJT**, what is the code for **COAL**? (________)

END OF TEST

/ 16

Test 10

You have **10 minutes** to do this test. Work as quickly and accurately as you can.

Each letter stands for a number. Work out the answer to each sum as a letter. Write your answer on the line.

Example: A = 1 B = 2 C = 6 D = 12 E = 10 D ÷ B = (C)

1. A = 5 B = 6 C = 8 D = 9 E = 12 A + E – C = (________)
2. A = 1 B = 5 C = 7 D = 12 E = 23 C × B – D = (________)
3. A = 2 B = 3 C = 4 D = 5 E = 8 E ÷ A + C = (________)
4. A = 2 B = 6 C = 8 D = 12 E = 48 E ÷ C × A = (________)
5. A = 2 B = 8 C = 9 D = 17 E = 25 A × B + C – D = (________)

Find the missing number to complete each sum. Write your answer on the line.

Example: 7 + 5 = 24 ÷ (2)

6. 18 ÷ 3 = 3 × (________)
7. 6 × 7 + 4 = 43 + (________)
8. 20 ÷ 5 + 8 = 4 × (________)
9. 9 × 3 – 2 = 100 ÷ (________)

The number codes for three of these four words are listed in a random order. Work out the code to answer the questions.

SEAT	ARTS	TSAR	RAVE
2413	1324	3156	

10. Find the code for the word **SEAT**. (________)

11. Find the code for the word **EARS**. (________)

12. Find the word that has the number code **5642**. (________)

Find the number that continues each sequence in the best way. Write your answer on the line.

Example: 3 6 9 12 15 (18)

13.	50	44	38	32	26		(______)
14.	17	19	20	18	23	17	(______)
15.	58	57	55	52	48		(______)
16.	36	36	38	31	40	26	(______)

END OF TEST

/ 16

Puzzles 3

These puzzles are an excellent way to practise your **numeracy** and **coding** skills.

Alien Arithmetic

Eric has been abducted by aliens. He can go back to Earth if he solves their maths problems. The problem is, he can't read alien numbers.

Each symbol corresponds to a digit 0-9. Use the sums on the right to work out which digits the symbols represent and fill in the table.

∴ =		★ =	
✚ =		● =	
⊘ =		⬢ =	
∓ =		⫰ =	
⦅⦆ =		◆ =	1

The Number Man's Plans

The number man eats letters and turns them into numbers. He has turned the three words below into number codes. Use the three clue words to work out the patterns in the numbers. Then, work out what the number man has said.

56485 **93877** **64757**

GLASS **RESTS** **TREAT**

3 4 5 5 4 6 7 **5 8 7 5 4** **9 6 4 8 5**

_ _ _ _ _ _ _ _ _ _ _ _ _ _ _ _ _ _ _.

Test 11

You have **10 minutes** to do this test. Work as quickly and accurately as you can.

Read the information carefully, then use it to answer the question that follows.

1. Aziz, Heledd, Richard, Laura and Elijah are comparing their scores in a spelling test. Richard got four questions wrong. Aziz got the highest score. Elijah spelt one more word correctly than Heledd. Laura scored 12/20. Heledd answered half as many questions correctly as Richard.

   If the statements above are true, only one of the sentences below **must** be true. Which one? Circle the correct letter.

   A Aziz spelt every word correctly.

   B Heledd spelt the fewest words correctly.

   C Elijah scored 10/20.

   D Elijah spelt more words correctly than Richard.

   E Richard got the third highest score in the test.

2. Alfie, Stacey, Juri, Dima and Aaron are talking about pets. Dima and Stacey both have 3 cats. Stacey has fewer fish than cats. Everyone except Stacey has a rabbit. Alfie has 2 guinea pigs and a dog. Juri and Dima have 2 dogs each.

   If the statements above are true, only one of the sentences below **must** be true. Which one? Circle the correct letter.

   A Aaron has more rabbits than Juri.

   B Stacey has 2 fish.

   C Alfie has fewer pets than Stacey.

   D Dima has more pets than Juri and Aaron.

   E Alfie doesn't have a rabbit.

Find the number that completes the final set of numbers in the same way as the first two sets. Write your answer on the line.

Example: 7 (4) 3   10 (5) 5   15 (11) 4

3. 7 (1) 6   7 (5) 2   9 (______) 3

4. 4 (16) 8   3 (9) 6   5 (______) 8

5. 18 (12) 2   36 (9) 6   42 (______) 6

6. 20 (5) 2   32 (4) 4   24 (______) 6

Find the pair of letters that continues each sequence in the best way. Use the alphabet to help you.

A B C D E F G H I J K L M N O P Q R S T U V W X Y Z

Example: TU   QR   NO   KL   HI   (EF)

7. JX   LZ   NB   PD   RF   (______)

8. EZ   GX   IA   KY   MB   (______)

9. ML   OK   RJ   VI   AH   (______)

10. BX   AZ   YD   VJ   RR   (______)

Underline the pair of letters that completes each sentence in the most sensible way. Use the alphabet to help you.

A B C D E F G H I J K L M N O P Q R S T U V W X Y Z

Example: **DG** is to **FE** as **RU** is to (TS SR TU ST US).

11. **GL** is to **CO** as **MK** is to (LN IQ IN IK GN).

12. **UJ** is to **OL** as **QM** is to (JO KQ MP JR KO).

13. **ME** is to **SF** as **NQ** is to (QU TR WR TQ WO).

14. **LQ** is to **JV** as **RP** is to (PU PS NU PW MR).

END OF TEST

/ 14

Test 12

You have **10 minutes** to do this test. Work as quickly and accurately as you can.

Find the number that continues each sequence in the best way. Write your answer on the line.

Example: 3 6 9 12 15 (18)

1. 6 12 24 48 (______)
2. 17 21 19 26 21 31 (______)
3. 30 28 27 27 28 (______)
4. 44 44 41 45 38 46 (______)

Underline the pair of letters that completes each sentence in the most sensible way. Use the alphabet to help you.

A B C D E F G H I J K L M N O P Q R S T U V W X Y Z

Example: **DG** is to **FE** as **RU** is to (<u>TS</u> SR TU ST US).

5. **HO** is to **GS** as **EV** is to (DW DY AB DZ DX).
6. **SY** is to **TX** as **PJ** is to (RH OH QK QI QJ).
7. **LH** is to **RO** as **RJ** is to (WQ UQ XO YR XQ).
8. **FA** is to **UZ** as **TE** is to (GT GV IU IV GW).

Find the missing number to complete each sum. Write your answer on the line.

Example: $7 + 5 = 24 \div ($ 2 $)$

9. $2 + 20 = 44 \div ($ ________ $)$

10. $27 \div 3 + 3 = 36 \div ($ ________ $)$

11. $10 \times 8 - 5 = 3 \times ($ ________ $)$

12. $24 \div 8 - 1 = 44 \div 11 - ($ ________ $)$

Each question uses a different code. Use the alphabet to help you work out the answer to each question.

A B C D E F G H I J K L M N O P Q R S T U V W X Y Z

Example: If the code for **MANY** is **LZMX**, what is the code for **GREY**? (FQDX)

13. If the code for **LIPS** is **HELO**, what is **XNKS** the code for? (____________)

14. If the code for **MINK** is **NLON**, what is **MRTH** the code for? (____________)

15. If the code for **MUCK** is **NFXP**, what is the code for **NILE**? (____________)

16. If the code for **CABS** is **YXZR**, what is the code for **VERY**? (____________)

END OF TEST

/ 16

Test 13

You have **10 minutes** to do this test. Work as quickly and accurately as you can.

The number codes for three of these four words are listed in a random order. Work out the code to answer the questions.

WITH THAW WASH SWAT
4316 1654 2451

1. Find the code for the word **WITH**. (________)
2. Find the code for the word **HITS**. (________)
3. Find the word that has the number code **1632**. (________)

Each letter stands for a number. Work out the answer to each sum as a letter. Write your answer on the line.

Example: A = 1 B = 2 C = 6 D = 12 E = 10 D ÷ B = (C)

4. A = 3 B = 5 C = 7 D = 12 E = 15 A + B + C = (________)
5. A = 1 B = 4 C = 5 D = 8 E = 12 B + C – D = (________)
6. A = 1 B = 2 C = 3 D = 7 E = 27 E ÷ C – B = (________)
7. A = 3 B = 4 C = 8 D = 9 E = 36 E ÷ D × A – B = (________)
8. A = 3 B = 8 C = 9 D = 17 E = 24 E ÷ A + C – B = (________)

Each question uses a different code. Use the alphabet to help you work out the answer to each question.

A B C D E F G H I J K L M N O P Q R S T U V W X Y Z

Example: If the code for **MANY** is **LZMX**, what is the code for **GREY**? (FQDX)

9. If the code for **TOUR** is **UPVS**, what is **GPSU** the code for? (__________)

10. If the code for **PLUM** is **KOFN**, what is **HLUG** the code for? (__________)

11. If the code for **SAKE** is **TCNI**, what is the code for **BANK**? (__________)

12. If the code for **AVOID** is **CSQFF**, what is the code for **CHOMP**? (__________)

Find the pair of letters that continues each sequence in the best way. Use the alphabet to help you.

A B C D E F G H I J K L M N O P Q R S T U V W X Y Z

Example: TU QR NO KL HI (EF)

13. ES IR MQ QP UO (_____)

14. WT XU YX ZC AJ (_____)

15. JU KT HS IR FQ (_____)

16. XW WU YR XN ZI (_____)

END OF TEST

/ 16

Test 14

You have **10 minutes** to do this test. Work as quickly and accurately as you can.

Find the missing number to complete each sum. Write your answer on the line.

Example: $7 + 5 = 24 \div ($ 2 $)$

1. $4 + 29 = 11 \times ($ ________ $)$

2. $10 \div 2 + 10 = 7 + ($ ________ $)$

3. $7 \times 8 + 4 = 120 \div ($ ________ $)$

4. $6 + 19 - 4 = 7 \times ($ ________ $)$

5. $55 \div 5 - 6 = 2 \times ($ ________ $) - 3$

The number codes for three of these four words are listed in a random order. Work out the code to answer the questions.

LOCK COIL ICON KILN

3154 1536 2364

6. Find the code for the word **LOCK**. (________)

7. Find the code for the word **NICK**. (________)

8. Find the word that has the number code **6354**. (________)

Underline the pair of letters that completes each sentence in the most sensible way. Use the alphabet to help you.

A B C D E F G H I J K L M N O P Q R S T U V W X Y Z

Example: DG is to **FE** as **RU** is to (TS SR TU ST US).

9. **TY** is to **VU** as **OV** is to (QO NO QS RP QR).

10. **GL** is to **ED** as **KZ** is to (HS JP IR FR IP).

11. **QJ** is to **XD** as **HN** is to (OJ NG PH OH QF).

12. **IV** is to **RE** as **TE** is to (FV IT FX GX GV).

Each letter stands for a number. Work out the answer to each sum as a letter. Write your answer on the line.

Example: A = 1 B = 2 C = 6 D = 12 E = 10 D ÷ B = (C)

13. A = 5 B = 7 C = 9 D = 11 E = 24 B × A – D = (________)

14. A = 3 B = 4 C = 5 D = 9 E = 24 E ÷ A – C = (________)

15. A = 2 B = 5 C = 12 D = 24 E = 60 E ÷ B × A = (________)

16. A = 3 B = 4 C = 10 D = 12 E = 14 D ÷ A + C – B = (________)

END OF TEST

/ 16

Puzzles 4

Time for a break! These puzzles are a great way to practise your **logic** skills.

Peter's Pastry Puzzle

Peter sells pastries in his bakery. He is not very good at keeping track of how many he's sold. Use the facts below to fill in the table for him.

- He sells fewer éclairs than sausage rolls.
- He sells four more éclairs than custard tarts.
- He sells fifteen sausage rolls.
- Cornish pasties are the most popular thing he sells.
- He sells two fewer éclairs than Cornish pasties.
- Custard tarts sell the least.

Pastry	Number sold
Cornish Pasties	
Custard Tarts	
Éclairs	
Sausage Rolls	

Codenames

Five top secret spies have disguised their names with codes.
One spy, known as **& # ! $!**, has been found out to be called **Clara**.
Match the other codenames to the spies' real names.

/ + # # *	**Henry**
£ + / $ *	**Ellen**
+ # # + /	**Nelly**
+ $ ^ & !	**Erica**

Test 15

You have **10 minutes** to do this test. Work as quickly and accurately as you can.

Find the number that completes the final set of numbers in the same way as the first two sets. Write your answer on the line.

Example: 7 (4) 3 10 (5) 5 15 (11) 4

1. 5 (2) 3 6 (3) 3 7 (______) 4
2. 4 (24) 8 10 (32) 6 10 (______) 5
3. 8 (14) 9 3 (1) 1 6 (______) 4
4. 3 (11) 30 7 (7) 42 6 (______) 18

Each question uses a different code. Use the alphabet to help you work out the answer to each question.

A B C D E F G H I J K L M N O P Q R S T U V W X Y Z

Example: If the code for **MANY** is **LZMX**, what is the code for **GREY**? (FQDX)

5. If the code for **FRET** is **COBQ**, what is the code for **RICH**? (__________)
6. If the code for **YELL** is **ZGMN**, what is **MKWG** the code for? (__________)
7. If the code for **MILK** is **PKOM**, what is **OCQM** the code for? (__________)
8. If the code for **HAWK** is **SZDP**, what is **OBMC** the code for? (__________)

Each letter stands for a number. Work out the answer to each sum as a letter. Write your answer on the line.

Example: A = 1 B = 2 C = 6 D = 12 E = 10 D ÷ B = (C)

9. A = 2 B = 6 C = 12 D = 24 E = 35 D – C = (______)

10. A = 1 B = 2 C = 8 D = 10 E = 11 E + A – D = (______)

11. A = 3 B = 7 C = 10 D = 12 E = 15 E ÷ A + B = (______)

12. A = 6 B = 8 C = 9 D = 12 E = 18 E ÷ C + D – A = (______)

Find the number that continues each sequence in the best way. Write your answer on the line.

Example: 3 6 9 12 15 (18)

13. 2 10 18 26 34 (______)

14. 33 35 31 29 29 23 (______)

15. 4 5 9 14 23 (______)

16. 41 46 50 53 55 (______)

END OF TEST

/ 16

Test 16

You have **10 minutes** to do this test. Work as quickly and accurately as you can.

Find the pair of letters that continues each sequence in the best way. Use the alphabet to help you.

A B C D E F G H I J K L M N O P Q R S T U V W X Y Z

Example: TU QR NO KL HI (EF)

1.	HX	DV	ZT	VR	RP	(______)
2.	OE	PA	QV	RP	SI	(______)
3.	SN	US	WW	YZ	AB	(______)
4.	EM	GP	HT	JY	KE	(______)
5.	AV	YY	ZA	XD	YF	(______)

Find the missing number to complete each sum. Write your answer on the line.

Example: $7 + 5 = 24 \div ($ 2 $)$

6. $14 \div 2 = 10 - ($________$)$

7. $8 \times 3 + 1 = 5 \times ($________$)$

8. $22 + 30 - 10 = 9 \times 4 + ($________$)$

9. $54 \div 6 + 2 = 36 \div 3 - ($________$)$

The number codes for three of these four words are listed in a random order. Work out the code to answer the questions.

MAUL LEAD DAME DUEL

5163 3641 4625

10. Find the code for the word **DUEL**. (__________)

11. Find the code for the word **MELD**. (__________)

12. Find the word that has the number code **4631**. (__________)

Read the information carefully, then use it to answer the question that follows.

13. Matt eats 4 pieces of fruit every day. On Monday, he eats 1 banana. On Tuesday he eats 2 apples. On Wednesday he eats 1 orange and 2 pears. On Thursday he eats more apples than on Tuesday. Friday is the only day he doesn't eat any bananas.

    If the statements above are true, only one of the sentences below **must** be true. Which one? Circle the correct letter.

    A Matt eats 3 pears on Monday.
    B Matt eats 3 apples on Thursday.
    C Matt eats 1 banana every day.
    D Wednesday is the only day Matt eats an orange.
    E Matt doesn't like pears.

14. Hillary is on a hike and is looking for a café to get a bottle of water. Her map is five squares wide along the bottom (A-E) and five squares high up the side (1-5). The wishing well is two squares northeast of the church. The enchanted wood is one square to the right of the wishing well. The church is in square A2. Three squares to the right of the church is a field of cows. The café is one square away from both the field of cows and the well, in column C.

If the statements above are true, only one of the sentences below **must** be true. Which one? Circle the correct letter.

A The church is next to the enchanted wood.

B The field of cows is three squares away from the enchanted wood.

C The café is one square away from the enchanted wood.

D Hillary must go through the field of cows to get to the café.

E The wishing well is northwest of the café.

END OF TEST

/ 14

Test 17

You have **10 minutes** to do this test. Work as quickly and accurately as you can.

Underline the pair of letters that completes each sentence in the most sensible way. Use the alphabet to help you.

A B C D E F G H I J K L M N O P Q R S T U V W X Y Z

Example: **DG** is to **FE** as **RU** is to (TS SR TU ST US).

1. **AP** is to **DQ** as **LH** is to (OK LK OI LI MH).
2. **AW** is to **HP** as **BN** is to (LG JD KH ID IG).
3. **YO** is to **XQ** as **LD** is to (NE KF MC KH KG).
4. **XO** is to **QL** as **TK** is to (MG MH ME OE NK).

Find the number that continues each sequence in the best way. Write your answer on the line.

Example: 3 6 9 12 15 (18)

5. 32 16 8 4 (____)
6. 5 8 10 16 15 32 (____)
7. 3 6 11 18 27 (____)
8. 12 16 22 30 40 (____)

Find the missing number to complete each sum. Write your answer on the line.

Example: $7 + 5 = 24 \div (\underline{\quad 2 \quad})$

9. $42 \div 7 = 2 \times (\_\_\_\_\_\_\_\_)$

10. $110 \div 11 + 10 = 7 + (\_\_\_\_\_\_\_\_)$

11. $20 \div 5 + 3 = 21 \div (\_\_\_\_\_\_\_\_)$

12. $14 + 11 - 9 = 2 \times (\_\_\_\_\_\_\_\_) + 2$

Each question uses a different code. Use the alphabet to help you work out the answer to each question.

A B C D E F G H I J K L M N O P Q R S T U V W X Y Z

Example: If the code for **MANY** is **LZMX**, what is the code for **GREY**? (FQDX)

13. If the code for **PUMP** is **RSON**, what is the code for **TUNA**? (________)

14. If the code for **CAKE** is **HVPZ**, what is **GDWY** the code for? (________)

15. If the code for **PAST** is **KWPR**, what is the code for **AUNT**? (________)

16. If the code for **TUTU** is **VXXZ**, what is **HHEW** the code for? (________)

END OF TEST

/ 16

Test 18

You have **10 minutes** to do this test. Work as quickly and accurately as you can.

Each letter stands for a number. Work out the answer to each sum as a letter. Write your answer on the line.

Example: A = 1 B = 2 C = 6 D = 12 E = 10 D ÷ B = (C)

1. A = 4 B = 6 C = 8 D = 11 E = 42 E ÷ B + A = (________)
2. A = 2 B = 3 C = 10 D = 25 E = 50 E ÷ C – A = (________)
3. A = 1 B = 6 C = 10 D = 12 E = 13 D ÷ B + C = (________)
4. A = 2 B = 3 C = 6 D = 12 E = 14 C × B + A – E = (________)

Each question uses a different code. Use the alphabet to help you work out the answer to each question.

A B C D E F G H I J K L M N O P Q R S T U V W X Y Z

Example: If the code for **MANY** is **LZMX**, what is the code for **GREY**? (FQDX)

5. If the code for **SODA** is **XTIF**, what is the code for **CUSP**? (____________)
6. If the code for **DASH** is **HWWD**, what is **JKPG** the code for? (____________)
7. If the code for **GULP** is **TFOK**, what is **HZOG** the code for? (____________)
8. If the code for **DENT** is **EGQX**, what is the code for **NUMB**? (____________)

Find the pair of letters that continues each sequence in the best way. Use the alphabet to help you.

A B C D E F G H I J K L M N O P Q R S T U V W X Y Z

Example: TU QR NO KL HI (EF)

9. NM OL PK QJ RI (______)

10. OD MB KX IR GJ (______)

11. WD XC AA FX MT (______)

12. MT NY QE VL CT (______)

Find the number that completes the final set of numbers in the same way as the first two sets. Write your answer on the line.

Example: 7 (4) 3 10 (5) 5 15 (11) 4

13. 10 (5) 5 8 (2) 6 9 (______) 3

14. 6 (9) 3 4 (16) 8 7 (______) 6

15. 9 (6) 2 4 (8) 6 9 (______) 4

16. 10 (2) 6 15 (4) 7 14 (______) 8

END OF TEST

/ 16

Puzzles 5

Time for a break! This puzzle will help you practise your **sequence** and **coding** skills.

Seeing Stars

Estrella Stargazer has made a map to help people find a new constellation. It starts on the star marked with the number 20 and follows the sequence +2, – 5. Shade the first 10 stars in the sequence to show Estrella's new constellation.

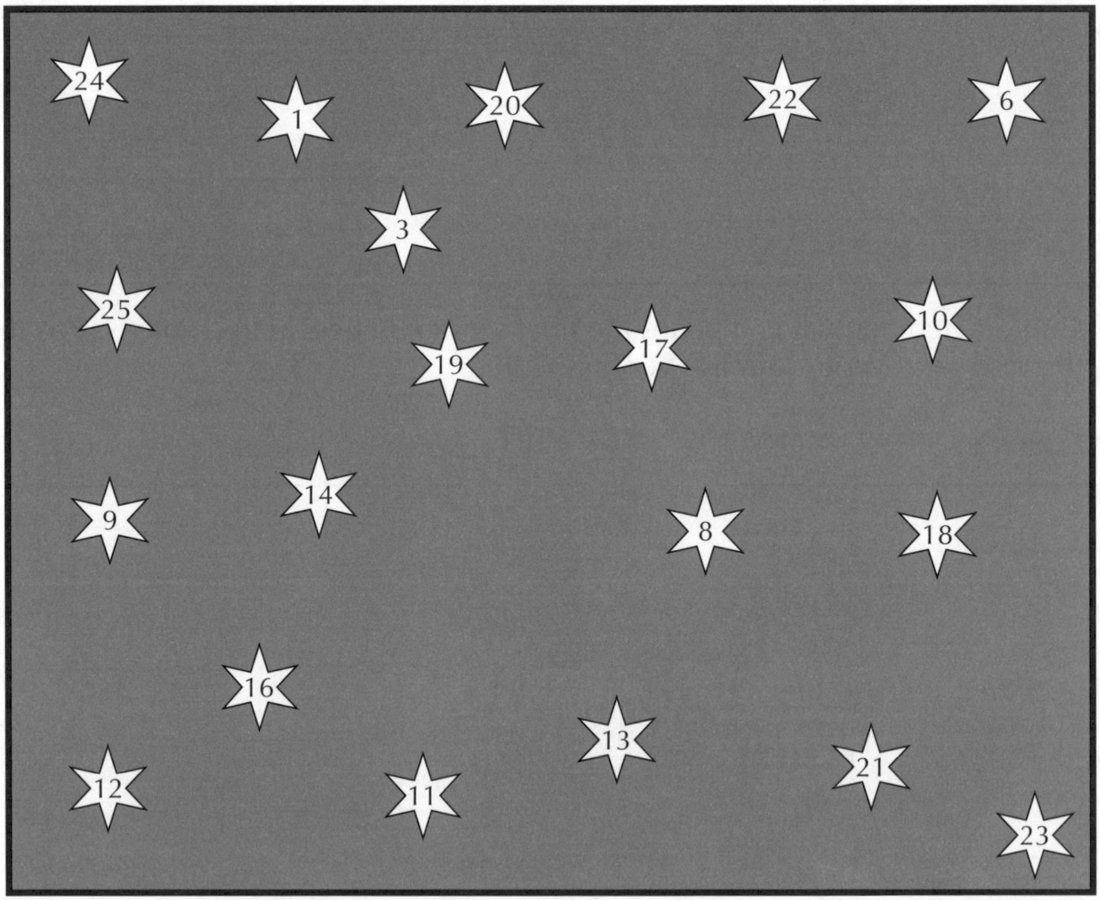

Work out the code to reveal the name of the constellation. Use the alphabet to help you. **A B C D E F G H I J K L M N O P Q R S T U V W X Y Z**

H K Z I P O R M T   U R H S

S P A _ _ _ _ _ _ _   _ _ _ _

Test 19

You have **10 minutes** to do this test. Work as quickly and accurately as you can.

The number codes for three of these four words are listed in a random order. Work out the code to answer the questions.

AMEN FLEA FLAN NAME

1352 6451 2135

1. Find the code for the word **FLAN**. (________)
2. Find the code for the word **FAME**. (________)
3. Find the word that has the number code **4512**. (________)

Each letter stands for a number. Work out the answer to each sum as a letter. Write your answer on the line.

Example: A = 1 B = 2 C = 6 D = 12 E = 10 D ÷ B = (C)

4. A = 3 B = 4 C = 5 D = 6 E = 12 C + B – A = (________)
5. A = 1 B = 2 C = 4 D = 10 E = 14 C ÷ B – A = (________)
6. A = 5 B = 6 C = 10 D = 11 E = 12 E ÷ B + C = (________)
7. A = 1 B = 4 C = 5 D = 10 E = 29 C × B + D – A = (________)
8. A = 2 B = 4 C = 5 D = 9 E = 10 E ÷ A + B – C = (________)

Find the number that completes the final set of numbers in the same way as the first two sets. Write your answer on the line.

Example: 7 (4) 3 10 (5) 5 15 (11) 4

9. 3 (12) 4 4 (8) 2 2 (______) 6

10. 7 (16) 3 6 (7) 2 4 (______) 5

11. 14 (6) 2 15 (4) 3 20 (______) 5

12. 3 (4) 9 2 (5) 8 4 (______) 8

Underline the pair of letters that completes each sentence in the most sensible way. Use the alphabet to help you.

A B C D E F G H I J K L M N O P Q R S T U V W X Y Z

Example: **DG** is to **FE** as **RU** is to (TS SR TU ST US).

13. **NQ** is to **MK** as **PI** is to (NC PC QZ OC OZ).

14. **OH** is to **SD** as **AN** is to (BI CM EJ EI EL).

15. **JI** is to **KF** as **OM** is to (PJ PM QK PH PG).

16. **JD** is to **ME** as **TG** is to (YF WJ UF WF WH).

END OF TEST

/ 16

Test 20

You have **10 minutes** to do this test. Work as quickly and accurately as you can.

Find the pair of letters that continues each sequence in the best way. Use the alphabet to help you.

A B C D E F G H I J K L M N O P Q R S T U V W X Y Z

Example: TU QR NO KL HI (EF)

1. VN YM BL EK HJ (______)
2. WR SW OA KD GF (______)
3. XY ZA DE JG RK (______)
4. BI DL HP JU NA (______)

Find the missing number to complete each sum. Write your answer on the line.

Example: $7 + 5 = 24 \div$ (2)

5. $15 - 4 = 44 \div$ (______)
6. $7 \times 4 + 1 = 41 -$ (______)
7. $9 \times 3 + 13 = 8 \times$ (______)
8. $99 \div 11 + 2 = 2 \times$ (______) $+ 3$

Each letter stands for a number. Work out the answer to each sum as a letter. Write your answer on the line.

Example: A = 1 B = 2 C = 6 D = 12 E = 10 D ÷ B = (C)

9. A = 1 B = 2 C = 3 D = 4 E = 5 E + B – C = (________)

10. A = 3 B = 4 C = 5 D = 12 E = 15 E ÷ A = (________)

11. A = 3 B = 5 C = 7 D = 16 E = 21 C × A – B = (________)

12. A = 4 B = 5 C = 15 D = 20 E = 25 D ÷ A × B – D = (________)

Read the information carefully, then use it to answer the question that follows.

13. Georgina, Alice, Freddie, Niall and Craig are giving each other gifts. Every person gives one gift and receives another. Freddie gives a t-shirt to one of the girls. Georgina gives Niall some chocolate. Craig receives a CD. Alice receives her gift from Craig. Alice does not give a CD to anyone.

If the statements above are true, only one of the sentences below **must** be true. Which one? Circle the correct letter.

A Niall gives his gift to Craig.

B Alice receives a t-shirt.

C Freddie does not receive a gift.

D Alice gives a gift to Niall.

E Niall and Georgina receive the same gift.

14. Ciaran, Waheeda, Louis, Ruth and Barbara are going into school in different fancy dress outfits. Each person arrives at school at a different time before school starts at 8:30am. Louis is dressed as a pumpkin and is the earliest to arrive at school. Ruth arrives twelve minutes after Louis at 8:24am. A vampire arrives seven minutes before school starts. A werewolf arrives before the vampire. The witch is the last person to arrive. Barbara is dressed as a ghost. Ciaran is the second to arrive.

If the statements above are true, only one of the sentences below **cannot** be true. Which one? Circle the correct letter.

A Ruth arrives after the werewolf.

B Waheeda is dressed as a witch.

C Ciaran is dressed as a werewolf.

D Waheeda arrives before Ruth.

E Barbara arrives at 8:20am.

END OF TEST

/ 14

Test 21

You have **10 minutes** to do this test. Work as quickly and accurately as you can.

Find the number that continues each sequence in the best way. Write your answer on the line.

Example: 3 6 9 12 15 (18)

1. 3 12 21 30 39 (______)
2. 49 48 45 40 33 (______)
3. 28 44 24 38 20 32 (______)
4. 24 8 12 4 6 2 (______)
5. 23 25 19 31 15 37 (______)

Underline the pair of letters that completes each sentence in the most sensible way. Use the alphabet to help you.

A B C D E F G H I J K L M N O P Q R S T U V W X Y Z

Example: **DG** is to **FE** as **RU** is to (TS SR TU ST US).

6. **XO** is to **ZN** as **VC** is to (XE ZY XY XB WZ).
7. **TQ** is to **NI** as **ZW** is to (RO TM TL TO TR).
8. **MB** is to **TA** as **SN** is to (AO ZM ZL ZJ XN).
9. **RM** is to **IN** as **UH** is to (EQ FT HQ FU FS).

The number codes for three of these four words are listed in a random order.
Work out the code to answer the questions.

IDEA FEAR ARID AIDE
1456 4561 3612

10. Find the code for the word **IDEA**. (________)

11. Find the code for the word **DIRE**. (________)

12. Find the word that has the number code **2145**. (________)

Each letter stands for a number. Work out the answer to each sum as a letter.
Write your answer on the line.

Example: A = 1 B = 2 C = 6 D = 12 E = 10 D ÷ B = (C)

13. A = 4 B = 7 C = 6 D = 28 E = 34 B × A = (________)

14. A = 2 B = 4 C = 7 D = 10 E = 20 D × B – E = (________)

15. A = 2 B = 7 C = 12 D = 13 E = 14 E ÷ A + B = (________)

16. A = 2 B = 7 C = 8 D = 10 E = 24 E ÷ C + B – A = (________)

END OF TEST

/ 16

Test 22

You have **10 minutes** to do this test. Work as quickly and accurately as you can.

Each question uses a different code. Use the alphabet to help you work out the answer to each question.

A B C D E F G H I J K L M N O P Q R S T U V W X Y Z

Example: If the code for **MANY** is **LZMX**, what is the code for **GREY**? (FQDX)

1. If the code for **SENT** is **PBKQ**, what is the code for **JUMP**? (__________)

2. If the code for **FOOL** is **HRQO**, what is the code for **JACK**? (__________)

3. If the code for **CASK** is **XZHP**, what is **HKRG** the code for? (__________)

4. If the code for **TOKEN** is **SMHAI**, what is the code for **GRAPE**? (__________)

Read the information carefully, then use it to answer the question that follows.

5. 100 animals escaped from a zoo. Half were zebra. 24 giraffes escaped. More flamingos escaped than antelope. The number of antelope that escaped was double the number of tigers.

   If the statements above are true, only one of the sentences below **must** be true. Which one? Circle the correct letter.

   A More than ten tigers escaped.

   B 13 flamingos escaped.

   C More than ten flamingos escaped.

   D More antelope escaped than giraffes.

   E Double the number of zebra escaped as giraffes.

6. Trisha and Millie are playing battleships. The board is four squares wide along the bottom (A-D) and four squares high up the side (1-4). Trisha has three battleships on her board, which Millie has to find. Each battleship is two squares long and can be placed on the board in any direction, except diagonally. Millie attacks square A3 and misses, but hits a boat one square to the right. C2 is also a hit. One square above is a miss. C4 is also a hit.

If the statements above are true, only one of the sentences below **cannot** be true. Which one? Circle the correct letter.

A C1 is a hit.

B A2 is a miss.

C D1 is a hit.

D D4 is a hit.

E B1 is a miss.

Find the number that continues each sequence in the best way. Write your answer on the line.

Example: 3 6 9 12 15 (18)

7.	64	32	16	8			(______)
8.	96	48	24	12	6		(______)
9.	47	52	56	59	61		(______)
10.	24	18	18	19	12	20	(______)

Find the missing number to complete each sum. Write your answer on the line.

Example: 7 + 5 = 24 ÷ (2)

11. 19 – 3 = 4 × (________)

12. 45 ÷ 9 + 1 = 14 – (________)

13. 4 × 9 + 3 = 49 – (________)

14. 16 – 11 = 24 ÷ (________) – 3

END OF TEST

/ 14

Puzzles 6

Time for a break! These puzzles are a great way to practise your **related number** skills.

Pompous Passcodes

Lord Pompous has just had a high-tech security system installed at his mansion, but he has forgotten the passcode to his puppy's playroom.

Follow the instructions below to help him work out the top secret security code. Write the missing numbers in each box.

- Each side of the rectangle should add up to 22.
- The blue boxes should also all add up to 22.
- The total of the white boxes is 33.

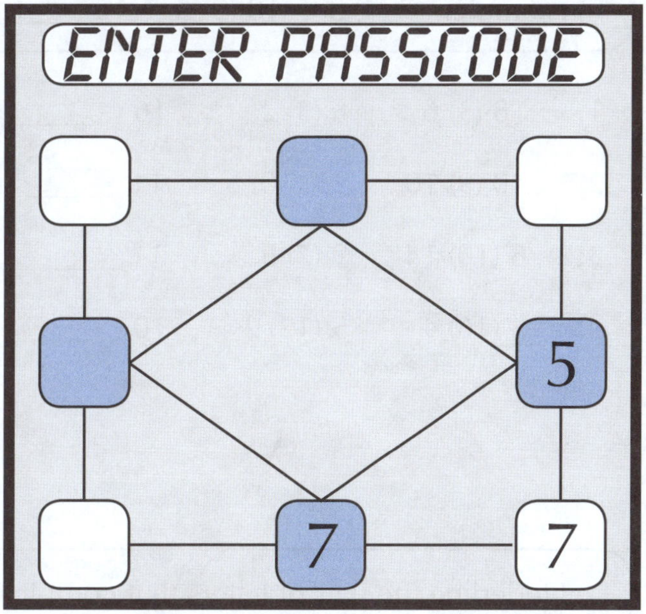

Frances's Fury

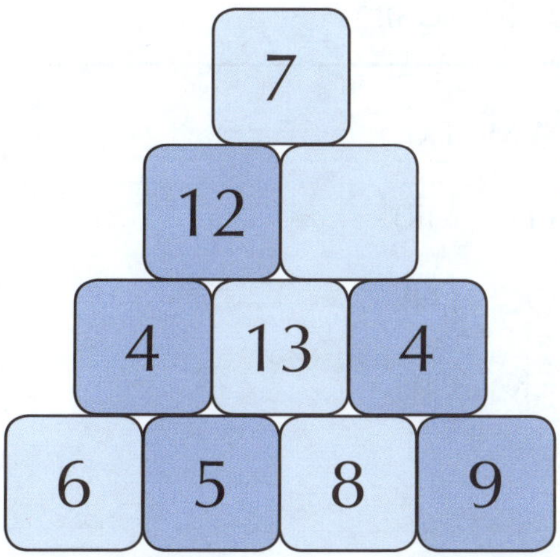

Queen Frances the Frog is furious. She has had a number pyramid built in her honour, but someone has stolen one of the numbers. Help her royal highness by writing in the missing number.

Test 23

You have **10 minutes** to do this test. Work as quickly and accurately as you can.

Find the number that completes the final set of numbers in the same way as the first two sets. Write your answer on the line.

Example: 7 (4) 3 10 (5) 5 15 (11) 4

1. 18 (3) 6 6 (3) 2 16 (______) 8
2. 40 (9) 10 25 (10) 5 4 (______) 2
3. 6 (10) 14 9 (7) 5 3 (______) 9
4. 3 (16) 4 5 (12) 2 10 (______) 4

Underline the pair of letters that completes each sentence in the most sensible way. Use the alphabet to help you.

A B C D E F G H I J K L M N O P Q R S T U V W X Y Z

Example: **DG** is to **FE** as **RU** is to (TS SR TU ST US).

5. **WS** is to **ZW** as **QG** is to (WK SI TM WM TK).
6. **MJ** is to **SB** as **FY** is to (NS LQ LS LT MR).
7. **XT** is to **TY** as **QB** is to (MG MI NH OG LH).
8. **WL** is to **DO** as **XR** is to (CH CJ EI CK CI).

Each letter stands for a number. Work out the answer to each sum as a letter. Write your answer on the line.

Example: A = 1 B = 2 C = 6 D = 12 E = 10 D ÷ B = (C)

9. A = 7 B = 8 C = 12 D = 16 E = 28 E ÷ A + C = (________)

10. A = 6 B = 10 C = 11 D = 13 E = 40 E ÷ B + A = (________)

11. A = 2 B = 4 C = 5 D = 11 E = 13 B × A + C – D = (________)

12. A = 2 B = 3 C = 7 D = 16 E = 23 B × C + A – D = (________)

Find the pair of letters that continues each sequence in the best way. Use the alphabet to help you.

A B C D E F G H I J K L M N O P Q R S T U V W X Y Z

Example: TU QR NO KL HI (EF)

13. SV RW QX PY OZ (______)

14. XN VO TP RQ PR (______)

15. BY CA FB GB JA (______)

16. GN HI JE MB QZ (______)

END OF TEST

/ 16

Test 24

You have **10 minutes** to do this test. Work as quickly and accurately as you can.

Find the pair of letters that continues each sequence in the best way. Use the alphabet to help you.

A B C D E F G H I J K L M N O P Q R S T U V W X Y Z

Example: TU QR NO KL HI (EF)

1. DJ EN FR GV HZ (______)
2. HW RA ZE FI JM (______)
3. GC IG ML SR AY (______)
4. HF FE FC HB LZ (______)

The number codes for three of these four words are listed in a random order. Work out the code to answer the questions.

FACE ACRE NEAR FERN

2431 6534 2654

5. Find the code for the word **NEAR**. (__________)
6. Find the code for the word **RACE**. (__________)
7. Find the word that has the number code **5624**. (__________)

Underline the pair of letters that completes each sentence in the most sensible way. Use the alphabet to help you.

A B C D E F G H I J K L M N O P Q R S T U V W X Y Z

Example: DG is to **FE** as **RU** is to (TS SR TU ST US).

8. **QT** is to **UZ** as **VH** is to (ZL CM XN XQ ZN).

9. **UX** is to **VW** as **JD** is to (HC ME KF KC KB).

10. **UM** is to **RT** as **EL** is to (YQ BU BS YS DS).

11. **XN** is to **CM** as **TF** is to (GS HS HT GW GU).

Each letter stands for a number. Work out the answer to each sum as a letter. Write your answer on the line.

Example: A = 1 B = 2 C = 6 D = 12 E = 10 D ÷ B = (C)

12. A = 6 B = 7 C = 9 D = 12 E = 42 E ÷ B = (________)

13. A = 1 B = 3 C = 5 D = 9 E = 11 B + E – D = (________)

14. A = 2 B = 5 C = 9 D = 10 E = 14 D ÷ A + B = (________)

15. A = 3 B = 5 C = 8 D = 9 E = 20 E ÷ B + C – D = (________)

16. A = 2 B = 4 C = 6 D = 22 E = 26 C × B + A – D = (________)

END OF TEST

/ 16

Test 25

You have **10 minutes** to do this test. Work as quickly and accurately as you can.

Each question uses a different code. Use the alphabet to help you work out the answer to each question.

A B C D E F G H I J K L M N O P Q R S T U V W X Y Z

Example: If the code for **MANY** is **LZMX**, what is the code for **GREY**? (FQDX)

1. If the code for **GRIP** is **ITKR**, what is **OKMG** the code for? (____________)

2. If the code for **WASH** is **VDRK**, what is **JHMW** the code for? (____________)

3. If the code for **EARS** is **IDTT**, what is the code for **NOSE**? (____________)

4. If the code for **PEACE** is **RFABC**, what is the code for **STONE**? (____________)

Find the missing number to complete each sum. Write your answer on the line.

Example: 7 + 5 = 24 ÷ (2)

5. 27 – 10 = 7 + (________)

6. 10 ÷ 2 + 5 = 50 ÷ (________)

7. 48 ÷ 8 + 4 = 2 × (________)

8. 18 ÷ 9 + 13 = 7 × (________) + 1

Find the pair of letters that continues each sequence in the best way. Use the alphabet to help you.

A B C D E F G H I J K L M N O P Q R S T U V W X Y Z

Example: TU QR NO KL HI (EF)

9. NH PG RF TE VD (____)

10. LX MY NA OD PH (____)

11. HD GF DJ CP ZX (____)

12. GK FJ GE JD OY (____)

Find the number that completes the final set of numbers in the same way as the first two sets. Write your answer on the line.

Example: 7 (4) 3 10 (5) 5 15 (11) 4

13. 4 (24) 6 2 (4) 2 5 (____) 6

14. 14 (35) 2 20 (10) 10 40 (____) 4

15. 8 (1) 6 7 (2) 3 7 (____) 1

16. 4 (20) 6 5 (26) 8 9 (____) 4

END OF TEST

/ 16

Test 26

You have **10 minutes** to do this test. Work as quickly and accurately as you can.

Find the missing number to complete each sum. Write your answer on the line.

Example: 7 + 5 = 24 ÷ (2)

1. 7 × 2 = 2 + (________)
2. 12 ÷ 6 + 15 = 4 × (________) + 1
3. 44 ÷ 11 + 11 = 30 ÷ (________)
4. 81 ÷ 9 + 9 = 10 × (________) – 2

Find the number that continues each sequence in the best way. Write your answer on the line.

Example: 3 6 9 12 15 (18)

5. 68 66 63 59 54 48 (______)
6. 35 19 11 7 5 (______)
7. 10 9 9 10 12 (______)
8. 18 12 19 18 20 24 (______)

Read the information carefully, then use it to answer the question that follows.

9. Kat, Josh, Will, Jeanette and Andy all have their birthdays in the same week. Each person's birthday is on a different day, apart from Josh and Kat. Will's birthday is between Josh and Jeanette's. Josh and Kat have their birthday on Wednesday. Andy's birthday is on Tuesday. Jeanette's birthday is after Andy's birthday. Will's birthday is not on Thursday.

If the statements above are true, only one of the sentences below **must** be true. Which one? Circle the correct letter.

A Andy is the youngest.

B Jeanette's birthday is on Friday.

C Will's birthday is before Andy's.

D No-one has their birthday on Sunday.

E Jeanette's birthday is at the weekend.

10. Last night, Ryan, Ben, Nathan and Andy spent all of their free time, between school finishing at 3:30pm and 8pm, doing their homework. Nathan did his between school finishing and football. Andy went to the swimming lesson from 5-6pm. Ben spent 3 hours on his homework. An hour after he came back from the swimming lesson, Ryan went to football practice for an hour.

If the statements above are true, only one of the sentences below **must** be true. Which one? Circle the correct letter.

A Ryan spent the shortest amount of time on his homework.

B Nathan was doing his homework at 7pm.

C Andy spent longer than Nathan doing his homework.

D Nathan did not spend as long as Ben on his homework.

E Ryan was doing his homework at 5:30pm.

Each question uses a different code. Use the alphabet to help you work out the answer to each question.

A B C D E F G H I J K L M N O P Q R S T U V W X Y Z

Example: If the code for **MANY** is **LZMX**, what is the code for **GREY**? (FQDX)

11. If the code for **NAPE** is **QDSH**, what is **IXHO** the code for? (____________)

12. If the code for **FUZZ** is **DXXC**, what is the code for **RAMP**? (____________)

13. If the code for **SKIN** is **TMLR**, what is **NKQH** the code for? (____________)

14. If the code for **TURF** is **GFIU**, what is the code for **DESK**? (____________)

END OF TEST

/ 14

Puzzles 7

Time for a break! These puzzles are a great way to practise your **sequencing** skills.

Alien Alphabets

Aliens have sent us a secret message, using a code based on two alternating sequences. Use the letters given in the table to translate their message into English.

English	A	B	C	D	E	F	G	H	I	J	K	L	M
Alien	H	Y	J	A	L	C							

N	O	P	Q	R	S	T	U	V	W	X	Y	Z

N P S L   B Z   J H K A F

___ ___ ___ E   ___ ___   C A ___ D ___

C I V Z Z   V O   D L   D P I I

___ ___ ___ ___ ___   ___ ___   ___ E   ___ ___ ___ ___

P K S H A L   L H O Q E.

___ ___ ___ A D E   E A ___ ___ ___.

Crocodile Creek

To cross Crocodile Creek, you'll need to use the number bridge. The crocodiles won't let you pass unless you fill in all the numbers in the sequence. Think about different number types — it might not be an obvious sequence.

Test 27

You have **10 minutes** to do this test. Work as quickly and accurately as you can.

Each letter stands for a number. Work out the answer to each sum as a letter. Write your answer on the line.

Example: A = 1 B = 2 C = 6 D = 12 E = 10 D ÷ B = (C)

1. A = 5 B = 6 C = 11 D = 12 E = 42 E ÷ B + A = (________)
2. A = 2 B = 7 C = 9 D = 11 E = 14 C + B – E = (________)
3. A = 3 B = 6 C = 9 D = 12 E = 18 E ÷ A + B – C = (________)
4. A = 3 B = 7 C = 9 D = 35 E = 48 D ÷ B × C + A = (________)

Read the information carefully, then use it to answer the question that follows.

5. Nigel, Lucy, Soraya, Maria and Sid are talking about which countries they have visited. Everyone but Sid has been to France. Only Lucy and Soraya have been to Spain. Maria has only been abroad once. Two people have been to Greece. Sid and Nigel have been to Germany. Nigel has been to three countries.

   If the statements above are true, only one of the sentences below **must** be true. Which one? Circle the correct letter.

   A Nigel is the only person to have been to three countries.

   B Maria has been to the fewest countries.

   C Sid has been to Greece.

   D Soraya and Lucy have been to all the same countries.

   E Nigel has been to Greece.

6. Barbara's sandwich shop sold 130 sandwiches in an hour. Tuna mayonnaise was her biggest seller. She sold 34 ham sandwiches. She sold 11 fewer cheese sandwiches than she did tuna. Cheese sandwiches were the second worst seller. She sold 25 egg and cress sandwiches.

If the statements above are true, only one of the sentences below **must** be true. Which one? Circle the correct letter.

A We cannot know how many tuna mayonnaise sandwiches were sold.

B She sold 32 cheese sandwiches.

C She sold twice the number of tuna mayonnaise sandwiches as egg and cress.

D She sold 41 tuna mayonnaise sandwiches.

E Half of all sandwiches sold were ham.

The number codes for three of these four words are listed in a random order. Work out the code to answer the questions.

GEAR EARN GAME RANG

4521 1234 4265

7. Find the code for the word **RANG**. (__________)

8. Find the code for the word **GERM**. (__________)

9. Find the word that has the number code **4126**. (__________)

Find the number that continues each sequence in the best way. Write your answer on the line.

Example: 3 6 9 12 15 (18)

10.	2	4	8	16	32		(_____)
11.	79	74	70	67	65		(_____)
12.	26	19	29	23	32	27	(_____)
13.	27	29	32	32	37	35	(_____)
14.	24	32	20	16	16	8	(_____)

END OF TEST

/ 14

Test 28

You have **10 minutes** to do this test. Work as quickly and accurately as you can.

Find the number that completes the final set of numbers in the same way as the first two sets. Write your answer on the line.

Example: 7 (4) 3   10 (5) 5   15 (11) 4

1. 6 (30) 5   6 (12) 2   2 (______) 2
2. 18 (12) 2   42 (10) 6   36 (______) 6
3. 6 (20) 4   3 (22) 8   5 (______) 2
4. 7 (4) 2   6 (2) 3   8 (______) 1

Underline the pair of letters that completes each sentence in the most sensible way. Use the alphabet to help you.

A B C D E F G H I J K L M N O P Q R S T U V W X Y Z

Example: **DG** is to **FE** as **RU** is to (TS SR TU ST US).

5. **GE** is to **FF** as **VL** is to (TL UO TK UM UK).
6. **QZ** is to **VR** as **SX** is to (WP XS XM VP XP).
7. **IU** is to **ES** as **ZF** is to (XD VG YB VD TA).
8. **NO** is to **UM** as **AM** is to (HL HK KJ EL HM).

Find the missing number to complete each sum. Write your answer on the line.

Example: 7 + 5 = 24 ÷ (<u>2</u>)

9. 12 + 14 = 42 – (________)

10. 64 ÷ 8 + 6 = 3 + (________)

11. 50 ÷ 5 + 2 = 2 × (________)

12. 63 ÷ 9 + 2 = 4 × (________) + 1

Read the information carefully, then use it to answer the question that follows.

13. Rory, Lucas, Damian, Ivy and Flavia are at an ice cream shop. They each buy 2 scoops of ice cream. Flavia buys 2 scoops of butterscotch ice cream. Lucas and Rory both buy 1 scoop of strawberry. Damian buys 1 scoop of strawberry and 1 scoop of mint. Three people buy 1 scoop of chocolate.

If the statements above are true, only one of the sentences below **must** be true. Which one? Circle the correct letter.

A Flavia is the only person who doesn't have a scoop of chocolate ice cream.

B Damian is the only person who has a scoop of mint ice cream.

C Lucas and Ivy have the same 2 flavours of ice cream.

D Rory has 1 scoop of chocolate and 1 scoop of strawberry.

E Damian doesn't like vanilla ice cream.

14. Buana, Nick, Sonia, Pete and Demi are counting insects on different parts of the school field. They count 135 insects in total. Demi and Nick count 30 insects each. Pete counts the most insects. Buana counts 15 insects.

If the statements above are true, only one of the sentences below **cannot** be true. Which one? Circle the correct letter.

A Sonia counted more insects than Demi.

B Pete counted 45 insects.

C Sonia counted 22 insects.

D Pete and Sonia counted 60 insects between them.

E Buana counted the fewest insects.

END OF TEST

/ 14

Test 29

10

You have **10 minutes** to do this test. Work as quickly and accurately as you can.

Find the pair of letters that continues each sequence in the best way. Use the alphabet to help you.

A B C D E F G H I J K L M N O P Q R S T U V W X Y Z

Example: TU QR NO KL HI (EF)

1. GA KB OC SD WE (______)
2. DS FQ JO PM XK (______)
3. RW PA NE LI JM (______)
4. HL IN LQ QU XZ (______)
5. LC PB TB XC BE (______)

Each letter stands for a number. Work out the answer to each sum as a letter. Write your answer on the line.

Example: A = 1 B = 2 C = 6 D = 12 E = 10 D ÷ B = (C)

6. A = 7 B = 9 C = 11 D = 17 E = 26 E – D = (________)
7. A = 1 B = 2 C = 7 D = 12 E = 21 E ÷ C – B = (________)
8. A = 1 B = 2 C = 3 D = 5 E = 15 E ÷ C – C = (________)
9. A = 2 B = 3 C = 6 D = 7 E = 13 B × A + D – C = (________)

The number codes for three of these four words are listed in a random order.
Work out the code to answer the questions.

WILT	**LIAR**	**TAIL**	**WART**
2136	**6315**	**4362**	

10. Find the code for the word **WART**. (________)

11. Find the code for the word **WRIT**. (________)

12. Find the word that has the number code **5136**. (________)

Each question uses a different code. Use the alphabet to help you work out the answer to each question.

A B C D E F G H I J K L M N O P Q R S T U V W X Y Z

Example: If the code for **MANY** is **LZMX**, what is the code for **GREY**? (FQDX)

13. If the code for **CHIP** is **BGHO**, what is the code for **FISH**? (________)

14. If the code for **VILE** is **THJD**, what is the code for **OPEN**? (________)

15. If the code for **OWLS** is **LDOH**, what is **GIVP** the code for? (________)

16. If the code for **CLUE** is **DNXI**, what is **OGZX** the code for? (________)

END OF TEST

/ 16

Test 30

You have **10 minutes** to do this test. Work as quickly and accurately as you can.

Find the number that completes the final set of numbers in the same way as the first two sets. Write your answer on the line.

Example: 7 (4) 3   10 (5) 5   15 (11) 4

1. 8 (17) 9   5 (8) 3   2 (______) 3

2. 32 (6) 8   18 (11) 2   21 (______) 7

3. 2 (6) 9   4 (8) 6   3 (______) 4

4. 4 (6) 2   8 (15) 3   9 (______) 5

Underline the pair of letters that completes each sentence in the most sensible way. Use the alphabet to help you.

A B C D E F G H I J K L M N O P Q R S T U V W X Y Z

Example: **DG** is to **FE** as **RU** is to (<u>TS</u> SR TU ST US).

5. **EO** is to **CU** as **TJ** is to (RS OS RP SN RR).

6. **UQ** is to **WP** as **GM** is to (IJ HO LO II IL).

7. **UL** is to **YN** as **KW** is to (OZ OY RW OX MW).

8. **ZP** is to **AK** as **HE** is to (SW SV SU QT RW).

Find the missing number to complete each sum. Write your answer on the line.

Example: 7 + 5 = 24 ÷ (2)

9. 54 ÷ 9 = 11 – (________)

10. 44 ÷ 4 + 8 = 13 + (________)

11. 36 ÷ 9 + 11 = 3 × (________)

12. 72 ÷ 8 + 2 = 32 ÷ (________) + 3

Find the pair of letters that continues each sequence in the best way. Use the alphabet to help you.

A B C D E F G H I J K L M N O P Q R S T U V W X Y Z

Example: TU QR NO KL HI (EF)

13. UQ ST QW OZ MC (______)

14. SS TR WQ BP IO (______)

15. PJ RK SM SP RT (______)

16. DX EY HU MV TR (______)

END OF TEST

/ 16

Puzzles 8

Have a go at these puzzles. They're a brilliant way of practising your **maths** skills.

Dot-to-Dot

The dot-to-dot below starts at the star and follows the sequence +4, -1, +4, -1. Connect the dots to reveal a picture.

Strange Sums

Something strange has happened to the sums below. All the signs have disappeared, and the answers have too! Work your way through the sums. Fill in each box with either a +, –, ÷ or × sign, and fill in each circle with the number made by each sum. For example:

2 [×] 6 = 17 [–] 5 (12)

15 [ ] 3 = 25 [ ] 5 ( )

11 [ ] 3 = 6 [ ] 2 ( )

4 [ ] 5 = 27 [ ] 3 ( )

24 [ ] 4 = 2 [ ] 3 ( )

Test 31

You have **10 minutes** to do this test. Work as quickly and accurately as you can.

Find the number that continues each sequence in the best way. Write your answer on the line.

Example: 3 6 9 12 15 (18)

1.	42	36	30	24	18		(______)
2.	94	93	93	94	96		(______)
3.	31	33	30	28	29	23	(______)
4.	32	31	16	30	8	29	(______)
5.	81	27	9	3			(______)

The number codes for three of these four words are listed in a random order. Work out the code to answer the questions.

ONCE MEND DONE OMEN

6325 4213 5423

6. Find the code for the word **ONCE**. (__________)

7. Find the code for the word **DEMO**. (__________)

8. Find the word that has the number code **1453**. (__________)

Each letter stands for a number. Work out the answer to each sum as a letter. Write your answer on the line.

Example: A = 1 B = 2 C = 6 D = 12 E = 10 D ÷ B = (C)

9. A = 4 B = 5 C = 7 D = 9 E = 28 A × C = (________)

10. A = 1 B = 2 C = 4 D = 8 E = 11 C + D – A = (________)

11. A = 2 B = 8 C = 9 D = 10 E = 16 A × C – E = (________)

12. A = 1 B = 2 C = 10 D = 11 E = 21 B × C + A – D = (________)

Each question uses a different code. Use the alphabet to help you work out the answer to each question.

A B C D E F G H I J K L M N O P Q R S T U V W X Y Z

Example: If the code for **MANY** is **LZMX**, what is the code for **GREY**? (FQDX)

13. If the code for **MAZE** is **IWVA**, what is the code for **WHEN**? (____________)

14. If the code for **VEER** is **SFBS**, what is **ZJQZ** the code for? (____________)

15. If the code for **BANG** is **YZMT**, what is the code for **HERD**? (____________)

16. If the code for **SCARF** is **QBASH**, what is the code for **TEMPT**? (____________)

END OF TEST

/ 16

Test 32

You have **10 minutes** to do this test. Work as quickly and accurately as you can.

Find the pair of letters that continues each sequence in the best way. Use the alphabet to help you.

A B C D E F G H I J K L M N O P Q R S T U V W X Y Z

Example: TU QR NO KL HI (EF)

1. FP HQ JR LS NT (______)
2. ET FW IZ NC UF (______)
3. TW YY CB FD HG (______)
4. YU ZS CN HL OG (______)

Read the information carefully, then use it to answer the question that follows.

5. Radek, Camilla, Asad, Sanjiv and Thea are playing a video game. They each started with 5 lives. 2 people have only 1 life left. Thea still has all her lives. Sanjiv has lost one more life than Camilla. Camilla has more than 2 lives left.

   If the statements above are true, only one of the sentences below **must** be true. Which one? Circle the correct letter.

   A Asad and Sanjiv have only 1 life left.
   B Camilla has 4 lives left.
   C Sanjiv has at least 2 lives left.
   D Radek has more than 2 lives left.
   E Camilla has the same number of lives as Thea.

6. Valter, Akan, Betsy, Michael and Jaya go to the fair. Everyone except Michael goes on the dodgems. Jaya goes on the most rides. Akan goes on one more ride than Betsy. Only Michael goes on the helter skelter. Only Akan and Valter go on the waltzers. There is also a roller coaster and a big wheel at the fair. Valter goes on one more ride than Michael.

If the statements above are true, only one of the sentences below **must** be true. Which one? Circle the correct letter.

A Valter goes on the roller coaster.

B Betsy goes on one ride.

C Michael and Valter go on the same number of rides.

D Jaya doesn't go on the roller coaster.

E Akan goes on the big wheel.

Underline the pair of letters that completes each sentence in the most sensible way. Use the alphabet to help you.

A B C D E F G H I J K L M N O P Q R S T U V W X Y Z

Example: DG is to **FE** as **RU** is to (<u>TS</u> SR TU ST US).

7. **VC** is to **NH** as **UG** is to (ML KJ PK JL MN).

8. **HS** is to **NM** as **JP** is to (PJ OI PG QH PK).

9. **GI** is to **AG** as **ZM** is to (TJ QL UK TK TI).

10. **GJ** is to **TQ** as **UW** is to (FC EC HF FD FF).

Find the missing number to complete each sum. Write your answer on the line.

Example: 7 + 5 = 24 ÷ (2)

11. 36 ÷ 9 = 21 – (________)

12. 25 ÷ 5 + 13 = 3 × (________)

13. 18 ÷ 9 + 10 = 36 ÷ (________)

14. 24 ÷ 3 + 12 = 100 ÷ (________)

END OF TEST

/ 14

Test 33

You have **10 minutes** to do this test. Work as quickly and accurately as you can.

Find the number that completes the final set of numbers in the same way as the first two sets. Write your answer on the line.

Example: 7 (4) 3 10 (5) 5 15 (11) 4

1. 2 (5) 4 3 (21) 8 5 (______) 9
2. 9 (15) 5 5 (5) 3 6 (______) 5
3. 20 (8) 2 32 (6) 4 28 (______) 7
4. 10 (20) 8 8 (40) 3 10 (______) 8

The number codes for three of these four words are listed in a random order. Work out the code to answer the questions.

PINK SNAP SKIN PAIN

6453 3524 3241

5. Find the code for the word **SKIN**. (__________)
6. Find the code for the word **PANS**. (__________)
7. Find the word that has the number code **6324**. (__________)

Each letter stands for a number. Work out the answer to each sum as a letter. Write your answer on the line.

Example: A = 1 B = 2 C = 6 D = 12 E = 10 D ÷ B = (C)

8. A = 2 B = 3 C = 9 D = 21 E = 27 C × B = (________)

9. A = 1 B = 2 C = 7 D = 11 E = 21 E ÷ C – B = (________)

10. A = 3 B = 4 C = 5 D = 6 E = 9 A × C – D = (________)

11. A = 3 B = 7 C = 12 D = 13 E = 14 B × A – E = (________)

12. A = 2 B = 3 C = 8 D = 10 E = 12 A × B + E – D = (________)

Underline the pair of letters that completes each sentence in the most sensible way. Use the alphabet to help you.

A B C D E F G H I J K L M N O P Q R S T U V W X Y Z

Example: **DG** is to **FE** as **RU** is to (TS SR TU ST US).

13. **EW** is to **HO** as **SP** is to (VJ VF VH VE TJ).

14. **UO** is to **QT** as **KR** is to (JZ DY GV GX GW).

15. **DR** is to **HS** as **ES** is to (KR IT IW JT GV).

16. **PX** is to **QR** as **JQ** is to (MK KJ NL KK HK).

END OF TEST

/ 16

Test 34

You have **10 minutes** to do this test. Work as quickly and accurately as you can.

Each question uses a different code. Use the alphabet to help you work out the answer to each question.

A B C D E F G H I J K L M N O P Q R S T U V W X Y Z

Example: If the code for **MANY** is **LZMX**, what is the code for **GREY**? (FQDX)

1. If the code for **SPAN** is **URCP**, what is the code for **FIND**? (________)

2. If the code for **DENY** is **FCPW**, what is the code for **BAWL**? (________)

3. If the code for **JAZZ** is **IAAB**, what is **OATV** the code for? (________)

4. If the code for **HUGE** is **JYMM**, what is **VMRB** the code for? (________)

Find the number that continues each sequence in the best way. Write your answer on the line.

Example: 3 6 9 12 15 (18)

5.	40	22	20	21	10	20	(____)
6.	49	44	38	31	23		(____)
7.	65	64	61	56	49		(____)
8.	46	48	43	46	40	44	(____)

Find the number that completes the final set of numbers in the same way as the first two sets. Write your answer on the line.

Example: 7 (4) 3 10 (5) 5 15 (11) 4

9. 5 (20) 2 2 (18) 3 4 (______) 5

10. 10 (1) 7 9 (6) 1 8 (______) 2

11. 9 (4) 8 9 (8) 4 7 (______) 5

12. 5 (16) 6 4 (15) 7 1 (______) 5

Read the information carefully, then use it to answer the question that follows.

13. Farmer Polly has 5 pigs. The heaviest pig weighs 24kg, which is three times as much as the lightest pig. The second heaviest pig weighs 18 kg. The third heaviest pig weighs an odd number of kilograms. Together, all 5 pigs weigh between 70 and 75kg.

If the statements above are true, only one of the sentences below **cannot** be true. Which one? Circle the correct letter.

A One of Polly's pigs weighs 11kg.

B The second lightest pig weighs less than 13kg.

C One of Polly's pigs weighs 16kg.

D The lightest pig weighs more than 9kg.

E Polly's pigs are all different weights.

14. Five children are discussing how much pocket money they get each month. Steph gets three times as much as Sam. Amala gets £10 a month. Lauren gets more pocket money than Amala. Zahir gets £30 a month. Sam gets the least pocket money.

If the statements above are true, only one of the sentences below **must** be true. Which one? Circle the correct letter.

A Zahir gets the most pocket money.

B Amala gets less pocket money than Steph.

C Steph gets less pocket money than Zahir.

D Lauren gets more pocket money than Steph.

E Amala gets the second smallest amount.

END OF TEST

/ 14

Puzzles 9

It's time for a quick break. This puzzle is a great way of practising your **riddle-solving**.

Pearly Problems

Dame Hedwig von Vassenhof has had her priceless pearl necklace stolen. She only left the room from 3-4pm, so this is when it must have been stolen. Read the witness statements below to find the culprit. No-one is lying.

The thief is: ______________________________

Prince Percy:
I was putting on my tights from 1-2pm. Then I went for a walk with Lady Lucinda for an hour. I spent the rest of the afternoon eating grapes.

Mystical Maureen:
I was making potions from 11am-12 noon. I cast an evil spell on Washerwoman Wendy while she was washing Prince Percy's tights. I spent the next hour cackling.

Lady Lucinda:
From 11am-12 noon, I had my harp lesson. Then I spent an hour eating cucumber sandwiches. An hour after I got back from my walk, I went shopping for cone-shaped hats.

Sir Victor Valient:
I spent this morning slaying dragons. I was polishing my armour from 2-3pm. Then I went to see Mystical Maureen for an hour to buy potions.

Groundskeeper Grimrod:
I was weeding the flowerbeds all morning. In the afternoon, I helped Sir Victor polish his armour. Then I went picking apples from the orchard for the next hour.

Washerwoman Wendy:
I made cucumber sandwiches for an hour before Lady Lucinda's lunch. I was washing Prince Percy's tights from 12-1pm. Later, I helped Grimrod pick apples from the orchard.

Test 35

You have **10 minutes** to do this test. Work as quickly and accurately as you can.

Find the number that continues each sequence in the best way. Write your answer on the line.

Example: 3 6 9 12 15 (18)

1. 35 31 27 23 19 (_____)
2. 72 71 68 63 56 (_____)
3. 24 14 26 11 28 8 (_____)
4. 2 3 4 6 9 14 (_____)
5. 16 5 8 10 4 20 (_____)

Read the information carefully, then use it to answer the question that follows.

6. Jemima, Elsie, Bob, Anwar and Theresa are baking biscuits. Jemima baked twelve. Elsie baked half as many as Anwar. Elsie and Theresa made the same number of biscuits. Bob baked the fewest biscuits. Anwar baked the second highest number of biscuits.

If the statements above are true, only one of the sentences below **must** be true. Which one? Circle the correct letter.

A Jemima baked the most biscuits.

B Theresa baked more biscuits than Anwar.

C Jemima baked twice as many biscuits as Theresa.

D Anwar baked six biscuits.

E Elsie baked twice as many biscuits as Bob.

7. Sarah is making drinks for herself and her four friends. One person has one sugar and two people have two sugars. More people want tea than coffee. Gautam drinks his coffee black. Anna likes her tea as sweet as possible. Lisa has the same drink as Greta, but with one more sugar. Sarah and Gautam do not have sugar.

If the statements above are true, only one of the sentences below **cannot** be true. Which one? Circle the correct letter.

A Sarah has coffee.

B Lisa has milk.

C Greta has coffee.

D Anna has two sugars.

E Lisa has tea.

Find the number that completes the final set of numbers in the same way as the first two sets. Write your answer on the line.

Example: 7 (4) 3 10 (5) 5 15 (11) 4

8. 40 (9) 8 20 (8) 5 21 (______) 3

9. 4 (20) 10 6 (6) 2 4 (______) 9

10. 3 (10) 4 2 (11) 6 5 (______) 8

11. 24 (10) 6 18 (9) 6 4 (______) 2

The number codes for three of these four words are listed in a random order. Work out the code to answer the questions.

EAST SALT SEAR RATS
4361 1356 2316

12. Find the code for the word **SALT**. (________)

13. Find the code for the word **REST**. (________)

14. Find the word that has the number code **1634**. (________)

END OF TEST

/ 14

Test 36

You have **10 minutes** to do this test. Work as quickly and accurately as you can.

Find the pair of letters that continues each sequence in the best way. Use the alphabet to help you.

A B C D E F G H I J K L M N O P Q R S T U V W X Y Z

Example: TU QR NO KL HI (EF)

1. QV PQ OL NG MB (______)
2. GG HI KK PM WO (______)
3. CN GM FK JH ID (______)
4. BD WF ZJ UP XX (______)

Each letter stands for a number. Work out the answer to each sum as a letter. Write your answer on the line.

Example: A = 1 B = 2 C = 6 D = 12 E = 10 D ÷ B = (C)

5. A = 1 B = 4 C = 9 D = 12 E = 15 B + D – A = (________)
6. A = 3 B = 5 C = 12 D = 15 E = 60 E ÷ B + A = (________)
7. A = 3 B = 6 C = 7 D = 13 E = 24 B × A + B = (________)
8. A = 1 B = 5 C = 6 D = 16 E = 18 E ÷ C × B + A = (________)
9. A = 2 B = 3 C = 4 D = 10 E = 14 B × C + A – D = (________)

The number codes for three of these four words are listed in a random order. Work out the code to answer the questions.

TREK ROTE POET PERT
1364 4265 1624

10. Find the code for the word **ROTE**. (__________)

11. Find the code for the word **KEPT**. (__________)

12. Find the word that has the number code **1325**. (__________)

Read the information carefully, then use it to answer the question that follows.

13. Carys has pet caterpillars. She gives them 100 leaves to eat. 1 of the caterpillars eats less than 20 leaves. Only 2 caterpillars eat more than 25 leaves each. The caterpillar that eats the most eats double the number of leaves than the caterpillar that eats the least. All of the caterpillars eat at least 15 leaves each.

If the statements above are true, only one of the sentences below **cannot** be true. Which one? Circle the correct letter.

A None of the caterpillars eat less than 17 leaves.
B Carys has 4 caterpillars.
C None of the caterpillars eat more than 38 leaves.
D One of the caterpillars eats 19 leaves.
E Two of the caterpillars eat 26 leaves.

14. Mohammed is travelling on the train from Soxford to Hancaster. The direct train takes 3 hours and 45 minutes. Trains that stop in Garrington take an extra 25 minutes. Direct trains leave on the hour every two hours, starting at 1 pm and finishing at 7 pm. Trains stopping in Garrington leave every hour from 11:30 am until 7:30 pm. Mohammed arrives in Hancaster after 8:30 pm.

If the statements above are true, only one of the sentences below **must** be true. Which one? Circle the correct letter.

A Mohammed catches a direct train to Hancaster.

B Mohammed catches the train at 3:30 pm.

C Mohammed catches a train after 4 pm.

D Mohammed arrives in Hancaster at 8:40 pm.

E The train Mohammed travels on stops in Garrington.

END OF TEST

/ 14

Test 37

You have **10 minutes** to do this test. Work as quickly and accurately as you can.

Find the missing number to complete each sum. Write your answer on the line.

Example: 7 + 5 = 24 ÷ (2)

1. 16 + 27 = 47 – (________)

2. 18 ÷ 2 + 7 = 2 × (________)

3. 28 ÷ 4 + 6 = 3 × 6 – (________)

4. 9 × 2 – 1 = 14 + (________) – 2

Underline the pair of letters that completes each sentence in the most sensible way. Use the alphabet to help you.

A B C D E F G H I J K L M N O P Q R S T U V W X Y Z

Example: **DG** is to **FE** as **RU** is to (<u>TS</u> SR TU ST US).

5. **RH** is to **NM** as **FJ** is to (AN DM BR EO BO).

6. **YV** is to **VQ** as **FK** is to (EI CH CF FI CG).

7. **EK** is to **CM** as **JW** is to (EZ HY GY HA KY).

8. **AZ** is to **ZA** as **KU** is to (NE PE NF PF RH).

Test 3 — pages 8-9

1. 4651
B = 4, A = 6, T = 5, S = 1

2. 5231
T = 5, O = 2, N = 3, S = 1

3. STAB
S = 1, T = 5, A = 6, B = 4

4. UM
The first letter in the pair moves back 2 letters. The second letter in the pair moves forward 1 letter each time.

5. ND
The first letter in the pair moves in the sequence +2, +3, +2, +3, +2. The second letter in the pair moves in the sequence +1, -4, +1, -4, +1.

6. SP
The first letter in the pair moves back 5 letters each time. The second letter in the pair moves in the sequence -2, -3, -4, -5, -6.

7. LC
The first letter in the pair moves in the sequence +4, +3, +4, +3, +4. The second letter in the pair moves back 2 letters.

8. 2
$18 + 17 = 35, 35 = 37 - 2$

9. 7
$35 \div 7 + 14 = 19, 19 = 12 + 7$

10. 8
$27 \div 3 + 9 = 18, 18 = 10 + 8$

11. 9
$36 \div 9 + 14 = 18, 18 = 2 \times 9$

12. 4
$17 - 9 = 8, 8 = 5 + 4 - 1$

13. KQ
The first letter in the pair moves forward 2 letters. The second letter in the pair moves back 4 letters.

14. DL
Each letter in the pair moves forward 3 letters.

15. ML
The first letter in the pair moves forward 1 letter. The second letter in the pair moves forward 8 letters.

16. EW
WZ and DA are mirror pairs, where the two letters are an equal distance from the centre of the alphabet. The answer will be the mirror pairs for V and D, which are E and W.

Test 4 — pages 10-11

1. 10
Divide the first number by the third number.

2. 9
Add the two outside numbers together, then add 4.

3. 3
Subtract the third number from the first number, then subtract 1.

4. 3
Add the two outside numbers together, then divide by 3.

5. 2536
G=2, O=5, L=3, F=6

6. 2134
G=2, I=1, L=3, T=4

7. LOFT
L=3, O=5, F=6, T=4

8. E
$4 \times 3 + 2 = 14$, E = 14

9. D
$40 \div 4 + 1 = 11$, D = 11

10. E
$2 \times 7 + 15 - 6 = 23$, E = 23

11. C
$24 \div 8 + 9 - 3 = 9$, C = 9

12. RO
The first letter in the pair moves back 2 letters each time. The second letter in the pair moves back 5 letters each time.

13. QK
The first letter in the pair moves forward 1 letter each time. The second letter in the pair moves in the sequence +5, +6, +7, +8, +9.

14. MM
The first letter in the pair moves in the sequence +2, +4, +2, +4, +2. The second letter in the pair moves back 1 letter each time.

15. VN
The first letter in the pair moves in the sequence -2, +5, -2, +5, -2. The second letter in the pair moves in the sequence +1, +3, +5, +7, +9.

16. TK
The first letter in the pair moves in the sequence +5, +6, +7, +8, +9. The second letter in the pair moves in the sequence +1, -5, +1, -5, +1.

Test 5 — pages 12-14

1. E
$10 \times 2 - 5 = 15$, E = 15

2. A
$7 + 10 - 12 = 5$, A = 5

3. B
$1 + 11 - 10 = 2$, B = 2

4. A
$18 \div 2 + 8 - 15 = 2$, A = 2

5. C
Helena had the ball at the start of the game. Gregory was the only person to never have the ball, so Helena must have had it at some point. No-one passed the ball to Helena, so she must have had it at the start of the game.

6. E
Some of his plans overlap with his plans with Miriam. He goes shopping with Lewis at 3 o'clock for double the amount of time he plays rugby. He plays rugby with Naseem for an hour and a half, so he must go shopping for three hours, until 6 o'clock. Johnny has planned to go ice skating with Miriam before 6 o'clock, so this overlaps with his plans with Lewis.

7. 3
Halve the numbers each time.

8. 38
Add odd numbers in ascending order: +3, +5, +7, +9, +11.

9. 79
The numbers follow the sequence −1, 0, +1, +2, +3.

10. 11
There are two sequences which alternate. In the first sequence, halve the numbers each time. In the second sequence, double the numbers each time.

11. YBXK
To get from the word to the code, move the letters back 3 letters.

12. MDTR
To get from the word to the code, move the letters in the sequence +1, -1, +1, -1.

13. WILT
To get from the code to the word, move the letters in the sequence -4, -3, -4, -3.

14. REAR
To get from the code to the word, move the letters in the sequence -2, -3, -4, -5.

Test 6 — pages 15-16

1. SAPW
To get from the word to the code, move the letters forwards 4 letters.

2. VEND
To get from the code to the word, move the letters in the sequence -1, -2, -1, -2.

3. TAXI
To get from the code to the word, move the letters in the sequence -4, +2, -4, +2.

4. MVCP
To get from the word to the code, move the letters in the sequence -2, 0, +2, +4.

5. 6
$110 \div 11 = 10, 10 = 16 - 6$

6. 4
$9 \times 10 + 5 = 95, 95 = 91 + 4$

7. 7
$32 \div 4 + 13 = 21, 21 = 3 \times 7$

8. 5
$8 \times 6 - 3 = 45, 45 = 9 \times 5$

9. PB
The first letter in the pair moves forward 4 letters. The second letter in the pair moves back 1 letter.

10. NF
The first letter in the pair moves back 5 letters. The second letter in the pair moves back 8 letters.

11. QW
The first letter in the pair moves back 2 letters. The second letter in the pair moves forward 6 letters.

12. MV
PS and KH are mirror pairs, where the two letters are an equal distance from the centre of the alphabet. The answer will be the mirror pairs for N and E, which are M and V.

13. 11
Subtract 7 each time.

14. 56
The number added increases by 2 each time: +2, +4, +6, +8, +10.

15. 12
There are two sequences which alternate. In the first sequence, subtract 6 each time. In the second sequence, add 1 each time.

16. 61
The number added increases by 4 each time: +4, +8, +12, +16, +20.

Puzzles 2 — page 17

Biscuit Thief
Tommy stole the biscuits. He claimed he was hanging the washing out, but Si said it was too wet to play football, so it must have been too wet to hang washing out. Si's statement is supported by Gaz's, who says that he was inside with Si.

Train Timetable

Service name	Bumblebury	Fendon-on-Sea	Headley Grove	Wallington Central	Breckham Parkway	Benthwaite
Wallington Wizard	11:10	11:17	11:24	11:31	11:38	**11:45**
Parkway Panther	11:45	11:54	12:03	12:12	12:21	**12:30**
Benthwaite Slug	12:08	12:13	12:19	12:26	12:34	**12:43**
Bumblebury Crawler	12:21	12:25	12:31	12:39	12:49	**13:01**
Headley Hopper	12:49	12:52	12:58	13:07	13:19	**13:34**

Test 7 — pages 18-20

1. PJ
The first letter in the pair moves back 4 letters each time. The second letter in the pair moves back 1 letter each time.

2. KL
The first letter in the pair moves back 5 letters each time. The second letter in the pair moves in the sequence −3, −4, −5, −6, −7.

3. XB
The first letter in the pair moves in the sequence +1, +5, +1, +5, +1. The second letter in the pair moves back 3 letters each time.

4. NY
The first letter in the pair moves in the sequence +1, +3, +5, +7, +9. The second letter in the pair moves in the sequence +2, +4, +2, +4, +2.

5. HL
The first letter in the pair moves in the sequence −2, −1, −2, −1, −2. The second letter in the pair moves in the sequence +5, +4, +3, +2, +1.

6. E
$3 + 8 - 1 = 10, E = 10$

7. D
$1 \times 3 \times 5 = 15, D = 15$

8. A
$15 \div 5 + 7 - 8 = 2, A = 2$

9. B
$2 \times 9 + 1 - 17 = 2, B = 2$

10. C
Gráinne raised the smallest amount. The smallest amount was £25 and Tim raised £80. Keith didn't raise the least amount. Waqar raised more than Keith. Louise raised more than Gráinne, so Gráinne must have raised the least.

11. C
Tasha cannot have a brother and a sister. Everyone but Perrie has at least 1 brother. Tasha has 2 siblings. She has more brothers than Raj, who has 1 brother, so she must have at least 2 brothers.

12. 1635
M=1, E=6, L=3, T=5

13. 1436
M=1, A=4, L=3, E=6

14. RATE
R=2, A=4, T=5, E=6

Test 8 — pages 21-23

1. 14
Add the two outside numbers together, then add 1.

2. 12
The answer is the midpoint between the two outer numbers.

3. 10
Add the two outside numbers together, then subtract 3.

4. 8
Divide the first number by the third number, then add 5.

5. VH
The first letter in the pair moves forward 1 letter each time. The second letter in the pair moves back 2 letters each time.

6. YK
The first letter in the pair moves forward 2 letters each time. The second letter in the pair moves back 4 letters each time.

7. RF
The first letter in the pair moves back 4 letters each time. The second letter in the pair moves in the sequence +5, +4, +3, +2, +1.

8. OQ
The first letter in the pair moves in the sequence +1, +2, +3, +4, +5. The second letter in the pair moves in the sequence −2, +1, −2, +1, −2.

9. D
$8 + 11 - 1 = 18, D = 18$

10. E
$10 + 11 - 8 = 13, E = 13$

11. B
$50 \div 10 \times 2 = 10, B = 10$

12. D
$30 \div 6 \times 7 - 5 = 30, D = 30$

13. D
Stuart's sunflower was the second smallest. Stuart's sunflower was double the height of the smallest, Tristan's, which was less than 1m tall. Therefore, Stuart's must be less than 2m tall. Dania's sunflower is 2.2m tall. Nigella's sunflower is 40cm taller than Stuart's. Katrina's sunflower is the second tallest, so it must be taller than either Dania's or Nigella's, both of which are taller than Stuart's.

14. D
A total of 10 people cannot have ordered steak. 6 people had pizza which means that 3 people had bangers and mash. 4 people had lasagne. Less people ordered fish and chips than bangers and mash, so either 1 or 2 people had fish and chips. There are 26 people in total. If 1 person had fish and chips, 12 people had steak. If 2 people had fish and chips, 11 people had steak.

Test 9 — pages 24-25

1. JV
The first letter in the pair moves back 8 letters. The second letter in the pair moves forward 2 letters.

2. DP
The first letter in the pair moves forward 3 letters. The second letter in the pair moves forward 6 letters.

3. RJ
The first letter in the pair moves back 5 letters. The second letter in the pair moves forward 8 letters.

4. LH
The first letter in the pair moves back 6 letters. The second letter in the pair moves forward 1 letter.

5. 48
Double the numbers each time.

6. 38
There are two sequences which alternate. In the first sequence, subtract 4. In the second sequence, subtract 5.

7. 53
The number added increases by 2 each time: +3, +5, +7, +9, +11, +13.

8. 66
The number added decreases by 1 each time: +5, +4, +3, +2, +1.

9. 9
$37 - 10 = 27, 27 = 3 \times 9$

10. 11
$9 \times 6 + 5 = 59, 59 = 70 - 11$

11. 3
$3 \times 4 + 12 = 24, 24 = 8 \times 3$

12. 4
$70 \div 10 + 15 = 22, 22 = 6 \times 4 - 2$

13. VANK
To get from the word to the code, move the letters back 4 letters.

14. BUZZ
To get from the code to the word, move the letters in the sequence -1,-4,-1,-4.

15. LIMP
This is a mirror code, where the letters are an equal distance from the centre of the alphabet. O is a mirror of L, R is a mirror of I, N is a mirror of M and K is a mirror of P.

16. FQBL
To get from the word to the code, move the letters in the sequence +3, +2, +1, 0.

Test 10 — pages 26-27

1. D
5 + 12 − 8 = 9, D = 9

2. E
7 × 5 − 12 = 23, E = 23

3. E
8 ÷ 2 + 4 = 8, E = 8

4. D
48 ÷ 8 × 2 = 12, D = 12

5. B
2 × 8 + 9 − 17 = 8, B = 8

6. 2
18 ÷ 3 = 6, 6 = 3 × 2

7. 3
6 × 7 + 4 = 46, 46 = 43 + 3

8. 3
20 ÷ 5 + 8 = 12, 12 = 4 × 3

9. 4
9 × 3 − 2 = 25, 25 = 100 ÷ 4

10. 4612
S=4, E=6, A=1, T=2

11. 6134
E=6, A=1, R=3, S=4

12. VEST
V=5, E=6, S=4, T=2

13. 20
Subtract 6 each time.

14. 26
There are two sequences which alternate. In the first sequence, add 3 each time. In the second sequence, subtract 1 each time.

15. 43
The number subtracted increases by 1 each time: −1, −2, −3, −4, −5.

16. 42
There are two sequences which alternate. In the first sequence, add 2 each time. In the second sequence, subtract 5 each time.

Puzzles 3 — page 28

Alien Arithmetic

∴ =	2	★ =	0
✚ =	7	● =	8
⦸ =	9	⬢ =	6
∓ =	4	⫯ =	5
⬬ =	3	◆ =	1

The Number Man's Plans

Glass = 93877
Rests = 64757
Treat = 56485
The number man says: **Letters taste great**.

Test 11 — pages 29-31

1. B
Heledd spelt the fewest words correctly. Richard got four questions wrong, so his score was 16/20. Heledd answered half as many questions correctly as Richard, so her score was 8/20. This is less than Laura's 12/20, Elijah's 9/20 and Aziz, who got the highest score.

2. D
Dima has more pets than Juri and Aaron. Everyone but Stacey has a rabbit, so Dima, Juri and Aaron all have a rabbit. Dima also has 3 cats and 2 dogs, so she has 6 pets altogether. Juri has 2 dogs, so he has 3 pets. Aaron only has 1 pet, a rabbit.

3. 6
Subtract the third number from the first number.

4. 20
Multiply the two outside numbers together, then divide by 2.

5. 10
Divide the first number by the third number, then add 3.

6. 2
Divide the first number by the third number, then divide by 2.

7. TH
The first letter in the pair moves forward 2 letters each time. The second letter in the pair moves forward 2 letters each time.

8. OZ
The first letter in the pair moves forward 2 letters each time. The second letter in the pair moves in the sequence −2, +3, −2, +3, −2.

9. GG
The first letter in the pair moves in the sequence +2, +3, +4, +5, +6. The second letter in the pair moves back 1 letter each time.

10. MB
The first letter in the pair moves in the sequence −1, −2, −3, −4, −5. The second letter in the pair moves in the sequence +2, +4, +6, +8, +10.

11. IN
The first letter in the pair moves back 4 letters. The second letter in the pair moves forward 3 letters.

12. KO
The first letter in the pair moves back 6 letters.
The second letter in the pair moves forward 2 letters.

13. TR
The first letter in the pair moves forward 6 letters.
The second letter in the pair moves forward 1 letter.

14. PU
The first letter in the pair moves back 2 letters.
The second letter in the pair moves forward 5 letters.

Test 12 — pages 32-33

1. 96
Double the numbers each time.

2. 23
There are two sequences which alternate. In the first sequence, add 2 each time. In the second sequence, add 5 each time.

3. 30
The numbers follow the sequence −2, −1, 0, +1, +2.

4. 35
There are two sequences which alternate. In the first sequence, subtract 3 each time. In the second sequence, add 1 each time.

5. DZ
The first letter in the pair moves back 1 letter.
The second letter in the pair moves forward 4 letters.

6. QI
The first letter in the pair moves forward 1 letter.
The second letter in the pair moves back 1 letter.

7. XQ
The first letter in the pair moves forward 6 letters.
The second letter in the pair moves forward 7 letters.

8. GV
FA and UZ are mirror pairs, where the two letters are an equal distance from the centre of the alphabet. The answer will be the mirror pairs for T and E, which are G and V.

9. 2
$2 + 20 = 22, 22 = 44 \div 2$

10. 3
$27 \div 3 + 3 = 12, 12 = 36 \div 3$

11. 25
$10 \times 8 - 5 = 75, 75 = 3 \times 25$

12. 2
$24 \div 8 - 1 = 2, 2 = 44 \div 11 - 2$

13. BROW
To get from the code to the word, move the letters forwards 4 letters.

14. LOSE
To get from the code to the word, move the letters in the sequence -1, -3, -1, -3.

15. MROV
This is a mirror code, where the letters are an equal distance from the centre of the alphabet. M is a mirror of N, R is a mirror of I, O is a mirror of L and V is a mirror of E.

16. RBPX
To get from the word to the code, move the letters in the sequence -4, -3, -2, -1.

Test 13 — pages 34-35

1. 4316
W=4, I=3, T=1, H=6

2. 6312
H=6, I=3, T=1, S=2

3. THIS
T=1, H=6, I=3, S=2

4. E
$3 + 5 + 7 = 15, E = 15$

5. A
$4 + 5 - 8 = 1, A = 1$

6. D
$27 \div 3 - 2 = 7, D = 7$

7. C
$36 \div 9 \times 3 - 4 = 8, C = 8$

8. C
$24 \div 3 + 9 - 8 = 9, C = 9$

9. FORT
To get from the code to the word, move the letters back 1 letter.

10. SOFT
This is a mirror code, where the letters are an equal distance from the centre of the alphabet. H is a mirror of S, L is a mirror of O, U is a mirror of F and G is a mirror of T.

11. CCQO
To get from the word to the code, move the letters in the sequence +1, +2, +3, +4.

12. EEQJR
To get from the word to the code, move the letters in the sequence +2, -3, +2, -3, +2.

13. YN
The first letter in the pair moves forward 4 letters each time. The second letter in the pair moves back 1 letter each time.

14. BS
The first letter in the pair moves forward 1 letter each time. The second letter in the pair moves in the sequence +1, +3, +5, +7, +9.

15. GP
The first letter in the pair moves in the sequence +1, −3, +1, −3, +1. The second letter in the pair moves back 1 letter each time.

16. YC
The first letter in the pair moves in the sequence −1, +2, −1, +2, −1. The second letter in the pair moves in the sequence −2, −3, −4, −5, −6.

Test 14 — pages 36-37

1. 3
$4 + 29 = 33, 33 = 11 \times 3$

2. 8
$10 \div 2 + 10 = 15, 15 = 7 + 8$

3. 2
7 × 8 + 4 = 60, 60 = 120 ÷ 2

4. 3
6 + 19 − 4 = 21, 21 = 7 × 3

5. 4
55 ÷ 5 − 6 = 5, 5 = 2 × 4 − 3

6. 6512
L=6, O=5, C=1, K=2

7. 4312
N=4, I=3, C=1, K=2

8. LION
L=6, I=3, O=5, N=4

9. QR
The first letter in the pair moves forward 2 letters.
The second letter in the pair moves back 4 letters.

10. IR
The first letter in the pair moves back 2 letters.
The second letter in the pair moves back 8 letters.

11. OH
The first letter in the pair moves forward 7 letters.
The second letter in the pair moves back 6 letters.

12. GV
IV and RE are mirror pairs, where the two letters are an equal distance from the centre of the alphabet. The answer will be the mirror pairs for T and E, which are G and V.

13. E
7 × 5 − 11 = 24, E = 24

14. A
24 ÷ 3 − 5 = 3, A = 3

15. D
60 ÷ 5 × 2 = 24, D = 24

16. C
12 ÷ 3 + 10 − 4 = 10, C = 10

Puzzles 4 — page 38

Peter's Pastry Puzzle

Pastry	Number sold
Cornish Pasties	16
Custard Tarts	10
Éclairs	14
Sausage Rolls	15

Codenames

/ + # # * = Nelly

£ + / $ * = Henry

+ # # + / = Ellen

+ $ ^ & ! = Erica

Test 15 — pages 39-40

1. 3
Subtract the third number from the first number.

2. 30
Add the two outside numbers together, then multiply by 2.

3. 7
Add the two outside numbers together, then subtract 3.

4. 4
Add the two outside numbers together, then divide by the first number.

5. OFZE
To get from the word to the code, move the letters back 3 letters.

6. LIVE
To get from the code to the word, move the letters in the sequence -1, -2, -1, -2.

7. LANK
To get from the code to the word, move the letters in the sequence -3, -2, -3, -2.

8. LYNX
This is a mirror code, where the letters are an equal distance from the centre of the alphabet. O is a mirror of L, B is a mirror of Y, M is a mirror of N and C is a mirror of X.

9. C
24 − 12 = 12, C = 12

10. B
11 + 1 − 10 = 2, B = 2

11. D
15 ÷ 3 + 7 = 12, D = 12

12. B
18 ÷ 9 + 12 − 6 = 8, B = 8

13. 42
Add 8 each time.

14. 27
There are two sequences which alternate. In the first sequence, subtract 2 each time. In the second sequence, subtract 6 each time.

15. 37
Add the two previous numbers together, i.e. 4 + 5 = 9, 5 + 9 = 14 etc.

16. 56
The number added decreases by 1 each time: +5, +4, +3, +2, +1.

Test 16 — pages 41-43

1. NN
The first letter in the pair moves back 4 letters each time.
The second letter in the pair moves back 2 letters each time.

2. TA
The first letter in the pair moves forward 1 letter each time. The second letter in the pair moves in the sequence −4, −5, −6, −7, −8.

3. CC
The first letter in the pair moves forward 2 letters each time. The second letter in the pair moves in the sequence +5, +4, +3, +2, +1.

4. ML
The first letter in the pair moves in the sequence +2, +1, +2, +1, +2. The second letter in the pair moves in the sequence +3, +4, +5, +6, +7.

5. WI
The first letter in the pair moves in the sequence −2, +1, −2, +1, −2. The second letter in the pair moves in the sequence +3, +2, +3, +2, +3.

6. 3
$14 \div 2 = 7, 7 = 10 - 3$

7. 5
$8 \times 3 + 1 = 25, 25 = 5 \times 5$

8. 6
$22 + 30 - 10 = 42, 42 = 9 \times 4 + 6$

9. 1
$54 \div 6 + 2 = 11, 11 = 36 \div 3 - 1$

10. 3215
D=3, U=2, E=1, L=5

11. 4153
M=4, E=1, L=5, D=3

12. MADE
M=4, A=6, D=3, E=1

13. B
Matt eats 3 apples on Thursday. He eats 4 pieces of fruit each day. Friday is the only day he doesn't eat bananas, so he eats a banana on Thursday. He eats more apples on Thursday than Tuesday, so he eats 3 apples on Thursday.

14. C
The café is one square away from the enchanted wood. The church is in square A2. The wishing well is two squares northeast of the church, so it's in square C4. The enchanted wood is one square to the right, so it's in D4. The field of cows is three squares to the right of the church, so it's in D2. The only place in column C that is one square away from both the wishing well and the field of cows is C3.

Test 17 — pages 44-45

1. OI
The first letter in the pair moves forward 3 letters.
The second letter in the pair moves forward 1 letter.

2. IG
The first letter in the pair moves forward 7 letters.
The second letter in the pair moves back 7 letters.

3. KF
The first letter in the pair moves back 1 letter.
The second letter in the pair moves forward 2 letters.

4. MH
The first letter in the pair moves back 7 letters.
The second letter in the pair moves back 3 letters.

5. 2
Halve the numbers each time.

6. 20
There are two sequences which alternate. In the first sequence, add 5 each time. In the second sequence, double the numbers each time.

7. 38
Add odd numbers in ascending order: +3, +5, +7, +9, +11.

8. 52
The number added increases by 2 each time: +4, +6, +8, +10, +12.

9. 3
$42 \div 7 = 6, 6 = 2 \times 3$

10. 13
$110 \div 11 + 10 = 20, 20 = 7 + 13$

11. 3
$20 \div 5 + 3 = 7, 7 = 21 \div 3$

12. 7
$14 + 11 - 9 = 16, 16 = 2 \times 7 + 2$

13. VSPY
To get from the word to the code, move the letters in the sequence +2, -2, +2, -2.

14. BIRD
To get from the code to the word, move the letters in the sequence -5, +5, -5, +5.

15. VQKR
To get from the word to the code, move the letters in the sequence -5, -4, -3, -2.

16. FEAR
To get from the code to the word, move the letters in the sequence -2, -3, -4, -5.

Test 18 — pages 46-47

1. D
$42 \div 6 + 4 = 11, D = 11$

2. B
$50 \div 10 - 2 = 3, B = 3$

3. D
$12 \div 6 + 10 = 12, D = 12$

4. C
$6 \times 3 + 2 - 14 = 6, C = 6$

5. HZXU
To get from the word to the code, move the letters forward 5 letters.

6. FOLK
To get from the code to the word, move the letters in the sequence -4, +4, -4, +4.

7. SALT
This is a mirror code, where the letters are an equal distance from the centre of the alphabet. H is a mirror of S, Z is a mirror of A, O is a mirror of L and G is a mirror of T.

8. OWPF
To get from the word to the code, move the letters in the sequence +1, +2, +3, +4.

9. SH
The first letter in the pair moves forward 1 letter each time.
The second letter in the pair moves back 1 letter each time.

10. EZ
The first letter in the pair moves back 2 letters each time. The second letter in the pair moves in the sequence -2, -4, -6, -8, -10.

11. VO
The first letter in the pair moves in the sequence +1, +3, +5, +7, +9. The second letter in the pair moves in the sequence -1, -2, -3, -4, -5.

12. LC
The first letter in the pair moves in the sequence +1, +3, +5, +7, +9. The second letter in the pair moves in the sequence +5, +6, +7, +8, +9.

13. 6
Subtract the third number from the first number.

14. 21
Multiply the two outside numbers together, then divide by 2.

15. 12
Multiply the two outside numbers together, then divide by 3.

16. 3
Subtract the third number from the first number, then divide by 2.

Puzzles 5 — page 48

Seeing Stars

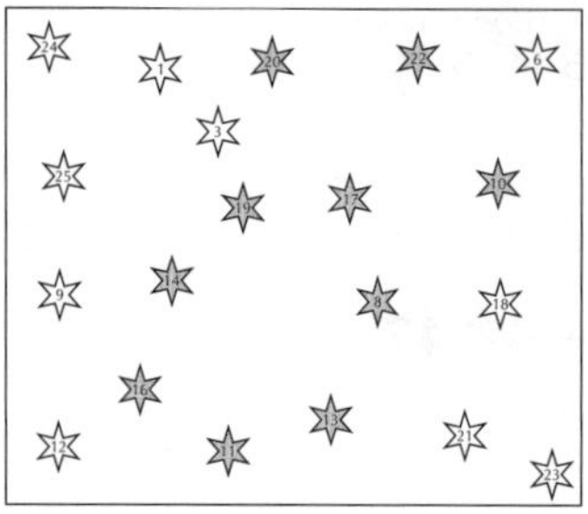

SPARKLING FISH. This is a mirror code, where the letters are an equal distance from the centre of the alphabet.

Test 19 — pages 49-50

1. 6412
F=6, L=4, A=1, N=2

2. 6135
F=6, A=1, M=3, E=5

3. LEAN
L=4, E=5, A=1, N=2

4. D
$5 + 4 - 3 = 6, D = 6$

5. A
$4 \div 2 - 1 = 1, A = 1$

6. E
$12 \div 6 + 10 = 12, E = 12$

7. E
$5 \times 4 + 10 - 1 = 29, E = 29$

8. B
$10 \div 2 + 4 - 5 = 4, B = 4$

9. 12
Multiply the two outside numbers together.

10. 15
Multiply the two outside numbers together, then subtract 5.

11. 3
Divide the first number by the third number, then subtract 1.

12. 3
Add the two outside numbers together, then divide by the first number.

13. OC
The first letter in the pair moves back 1 letter.
The second letter in the pair moves back 6 letters.

14. EJ
The first letter in the pair moves forward 4 letters.
The second letter in the pair moves back 4 letters.

15. PJ
The first letter in the pair moves forward 1 letter.
The second letter in the pair moves back 3 letters.

16. WH
The first letter in the pair moves forward 3 letters.
The second letter in the pair moves forward 1 letter.

Test 20 — pages 51-53

1. KI
The first letter in the pair moves forward 3 letters each time. The second letter in the pair moves back 1 letter each time.

2. CG
The first letter in the pair moves back 4 letters each time. The second letter in the pair moves in the sequence +5, +4, +3, +2, +1.

3. BM
The first letter in the pair moves in the sequence +2, +4, +6, +8, +10. The second letter in the pair moves in the sequence +2, +4, +2, +4, +2.

4. PH
The first letter in the pair moves in the sequence +2, +4, +2, +4, +2. The second letter in the pair moves in the sequence +3, +4, +5, +6, +7.

5. 4
$15 - 4 = 11, 11 = 44 \div 4$

6. 12
$7 \times 4 + 1 = 29, 29 = 41 - 12$

7. 5
$9 \times 3 + 13 = 40, 40 = 8 \times 5$

8. 4
$99 \div 11 + 2 = 11, 11 = 2 \times 4 + 3$

9. D
$5 + 2 - 3 = 4, D = 4$

10. C
$15 \div 3 = 5, C = 5$

11. D
$7 \times 3 - 5 = 16, D = 16$

12. B
$20 \div 4 \times 5 - 20 = 5, B = 5$

13. A
Niall gives his gift to Craig. Georgina gives her gift to Niall, Craig gives his gift to Alice and Freddie gives his gift to Georgina (the only other girl). This leaves only Niall and Alice who have not given a gift. Craig receives a CD, but Alice does not give a CD, so it must be Niall who gave Craig the CD.

14. B
Waheeda cannot be dressed as a witch. Louis is first to arrive and Ciaran is second. A vampire arrives at 8:23am. A werewolf arrives before the vampire, so the werewolf is Ciaran, as Barbara is a ghost. Ruth arrives after the vampire at 8:24am. The witch arrives last, so Ruth must be dressed as a witch. This means Waheeda must be the vampire.

Test 21 — pages 54-55

1. 48
Add 9 each time.

2. 24
The number subtracted increases by 2 each time: −1, −3, −5, −7, −9.

3. 16
There are two sequences which alternate. In the first sequence, subtract 4 each time. In the second sequence, subtract 6 each time.

4. 3
There are two sequences which alternate. In the first sequence, halve the numbers each time. In the second sequence, halve the numbers each time.

5. 11
There are two sequences which alternate. In the first sequence, subtract 4 each time. In the second sequence, add 6 each time.

6. XB
The first letter in the pair moves forward 2 letters. The second letter in the pair moves back 1 letter.

7. TO
The first letter in the pair moves back 6 letters. The second letter in the pair moves back 8 letters.

8. ZM
The first letter in the pair moves forward 7 letters. The second letter in the pair moves back 1 letter.

9. FS
RM and IN are mirror pairs, where the two letters are an equal distance from the centre of the alphabet. The answer will be the mirror pairs for U and H, which are F and S.

10. 4561
I=4, D=5, E=6, A=1

11. 5426
D=5, I=4, R=2, E=6

12. RAID
R=2, A=1, I=4, D=5

13. D
$7 \times 4 = 28, D = 28$

14. E
$10 \times 4 - 20 = 20, E = 20$

15. E
$14 \div 2 + 7 = 14, E = 14$

16. C
$24 \div 8 + 7 - 2 = 8, C = 8$

Test 22 — pages 56-58

1. GRJM
To get from the word to the code, move the letters back 3 letters.

2. LDEN
To get from the word to the code, move the letters in the sequence +2, +3, +2, +3.

3. SPIT
This is a mirror code, where the letters are an equal distance from the centre of the alphabet. H is a mirror of S, K is a mirror of P, R is a mirror of I and G is a mirror of T.

4. FPXLZ
To get from the word to the code, move the letters in the sequence -1, -2, -3, -4, -5.

5. C
More than ten flamingos escaped. Half of 100 is 50, so 50 zebra escaped. If 50 of the 100 escaped animals are zebra and 24 are giraffes, 26 other animals escaped from the zoo. To make 26, five tigers must have escaped, ten antelope must have escaped and therefore eleven flamingos escaped.

6. C
D1 cannot be a hit. There are hits in C2 and C4 and a hit one square to the right of A3, in B3. None of these hits are next to each other, so they must be three different boats. As the boats are all two squares long, hits must be in squares that are directly next to another hit. D1 is not next to C2, C4 or B3, so it cannot be a hit.

7. 4
Halve the numbers each time.

8. 3
Halve the numbers each time.

9. 62
The number added decreases by 1 each time: +5, +4, +3, +2, +1.

10. 6
There are two sequences which alternate. In the first sequence, subtract 6 each time. In the second sequence, add 1 each time.

11. 4
$19 - 3 = 16, 16 = 4 \times 4$

12. 8
$45 \div 9 + 1 = 6, 6 = 14 - 8$

13. 10
$4 \times 9 + 3 = 39, 39 = 49 - 10$

14. 3
$16 - 11 = 5, 5 = 24 \div 3 - 3$

Puzzles 6 — page 59

Pompous Passwords

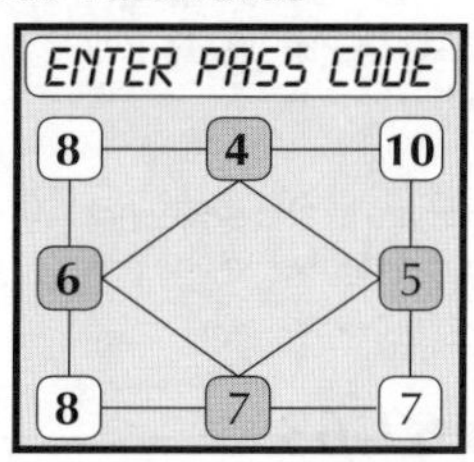

Frances's Fury

The missing number is 2. The total of each row on the pyramid increases by 7 each time, so the second row must equal 14.

Test 23 — pages 60-61

1. 2
Divide the first number by the third number.

2. 7
Divide the first number by the third number, then add 5.

3. 6
The answer is the midpoint between the two numbers.

4. 44
Multiply the two outside numbers together, then add the third number.

5. TK
The first letter in the pair moves forward 3 letters. The second letter in the pair moves forward 4 letters.

6. LQ
The first letter in the pair moves forward 6 letters. The second letter in the pair moves back 8 letters.

7. MG
The first letter in the pair moves back 4 letters. The second letter in the pair moves forward 5 letters.

8. CI
WL and DO are mirror pairs, where the two letters are an equal distance from the centre of the alphabet. The answer will be the mirror pairs for X and R, which are C and I.

9. D
$28 \div 7 + 12 = 16, D = 16$

10. B
$40 \div 10 + 6 = 10, B = 10$

11. A
$4 \times 2 + 5 - 11 = 2, A = 2$

12. C
$3 \times 7 + 2 - 16 = 7, C = 7$

13. NA
The first letter in the pair moves back 1 letter each time. The second letter in the pair moves forward 1 letter each time.

14. NS
The first letter in the pair moves back 2 letters each time. The second letter in the pair moves forward 1 letter each time.

15. KY
The first letter in the pair moves in the sequence +1, +3, +1, +3, +1. The second letter in the pair moves in the sequence +2, +1, 0, −1, −2.

16. VY
The first letter in the pair moves in the sequence +1, +2, +3, +4, +5. The second letter in the pair moves in the sequence −5, −4, −3, −2, −1.

Test 24 — pages 62-63

1. ID
The first letter in the pair moves forward 1 letter each time. The second letter in the pair moves forward 4 letters each time.

2. LQ
The first letter in the pair moves in the sequence +10, +8, +6, +4, +2. The second letter in the pair moves forward 4 letters each time.

3. KG
The first letter in the pair moves in the sequence +2, +4, +6, +8, +10. The second letter in the pair moves in the sequence +4, +5, +6, +7, +8.

4. RY
The first letter in the pair moves in the sequence −2, 0, +2, +4, +6. The second letter in the pair moves in the sequence −1, −2, −1, −2, −1.

5. 1463
N=1, E=4, A=6, R=3

6. 3654
R=3, A=6, C=5, E=4

7. CAFE
C=5, A=6, F=2, E=4

8. ZN
The first letter in the pair moves forward 4 letters. The second letter in the pair moves forward 6 letters.

9. KC
The first letter in the pair moves forward 1 letter. The second letter in the pair moves back 1 letter.

10. BS
The first letter in the pair moves back 3 letters. The second letter in the pair moves forward 7 letters.

11. GU
XN and CM are mirror pairs, where the two letters are an equal distance from the centre of the alphabet. The answer will be the mirror pairs for T and F, which are G and U.

12. A
$42 \div 7 = 6, A = 6$

13. C
$3 + 11 - 9 = 5, C = 5$

14. D
$10 \div 2 + 5 = 10, D = 10$

15. A
$20 \div 5 + 8 - 9 = 3, A = 3$

16. B
$6 \times 4 + 2 - 22 = 4, B = 4$

Test 25 — pages 64-65

1. MIKE
To get from the code to the word, move the letters back 2 letters.

2. KENT
To get from the code to the word, move the letters in the sequence +1, -3, +1, -3.

3. RRUF
To get from the word to the code, move the letters in the sequence +4, +3, +2, +1.

4. UUOMC
To get from the word to the code, move the letters in the sequence +2, +1, 0, -1, -2.

5. 10
27 − 10 = 17, 17 = 7 + 10

6. 5
10 ÷ 2 + 5 = 10, 10 = 50 ÷ 5

7. 5
48 ÷ 8 + 4 = 10, 10 = 2 × 5

8. 2
18 ÷ 9 + 13 = 15, 15 = 7 × 2 + 1

9. XC
The first letter in the pair moves forward 2 letters. The second letter in the pair moves back 1 letter each time.

10. QM
The first letter in the pair moves forward 1 letter each time. The second letter in the pair moves in the sequence +1, +2, +3, +4, +5.

11. YH
The first letter in the pair moves in the sequence −1, −3, −1, −3, −1. The second letter in the pair moves in the sequence +2, +4, +6, +8, +10.

12. VX
The first letter in the pair moves in the sequence −1, +1, +3, +5, +7. The second letter in the pair moves in the sequence −1, −5, −1, −5, −1.

13. 30
Multiply the two outside numbers together.

14. 50
Divide the first number by the third number, then multiply by 5.

15. 3
Subtract the third number from the first number, then divide by 2.

16. 26
Add the two outside numbers together, then multiply by 2.

Test 26 — pages 66-68

1. 12
7 × 2 = 14, 14 = 2 + 12

2. 4
12 ÷ 6 + 15 = 17, 17 = 4 × 4 + 1

3. 2
44 ÷ 11 + 11 = 15, 15 = 30 ÷ 2

4. 2
81 ÷ 9 + 9 = 18, 18 = 10 × 2 − 2

5. 41
The number subtracted increases by 1 each time: −2, −3, −4, −5, −6, −7.

6. 4
The number subtracted halves each time: −16, −8, −4, −2, −1.

7. 15
The numbers follow the sequence −1, 0, +1, +2, +3.

8. 21
There are two sequences which alternate. In the first sequence, add 1 each time. In the second sequence, add 6 each time.

9. E
Jeanette's birthday is at the weekend. Her birthday is after Andy's, so it must be on Thursday or afterwards, as it is Kat and Josh's birthday on Wednesday and no-one else shares a birthday. Will's birthday is in between Josh and Jeanette's birthday, but not on Thursday, so it must be on Friday or Saturday. Therefore, Jeanette's birthday must be on Saturday or Sunday.

10. A
Ryan spent the shortest amount of time on his homework. Ryan went to swimming and football practice. As both lasted an hour, he only had 2.5 hours to spend on his homework. Nathan and Andy only went to either swimming or football, so they had 3.5 hours to spend on their homework. Ben spent 3 hours on his homework.

11. FUEL
To get from the code to the word, move the letters back 3 letters.

12. PDKS
To get from the word to the code, move the letters in the sequence -2, +3, -2, +3.

13. MIND
To get from the code to the word, move the letters in the sequence -1, -2, -3, -4.

14. WVHP
This is a mirror code, where the letters are an equal distance from the centre of the alphabet. D is a mirror of W, E is a mirror of V, S is a mirror of H and K is a mirror of P.

Puzzles 7 — page 69

Alien Alphabets

There are two sequences which alternate. In the first sequence, move the letters forward 7 letters. In the second sequence, move the letters back 3 letters.

English	A	B	C	D	E	F	G	H	I	J	K	L	M
Alien	H	Y	J	A	L	C	N	E	P	G	R	I	T

N	O	P	Q	R	S	T	U	V	W	X	Y	Z
K	V	M	X	O	Z	Q	B	S	D	U	F	W

GIVE US CANDY FLOSS OR WE WILL INVADE EARTH.

Crocodile Creek

The numbers increase by square numbers, +1, +4, +9, +16, +25, +36.

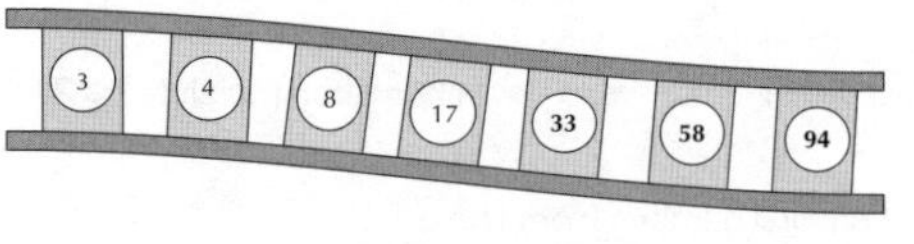

Test 27 — pages 70-72

1. D
42 ÷ 6 + 5 = 12, D = 12

2. A
9 + 7 − 14 = 2, A = 2

3. A
18 ÷ 3 + 6 − 9 = 3, A = 3

4. E
35 ÷ 7 × 9 + 3 = 48, E = 48

5. E
Nigel has been to Greece. He has been to three countries and we know that Germany is one of them. Everyone but Sid has been to France, so Nigel has also been to France. Only Soraya and Lucy have been to Spain so we know that he is one of the two people who have been to Greece.

6. D
Barbara sold 41 tuna mayonnaise sandwiches. She sold 25 egg and cress sandwiches and 34 ham sandwiches, so 71 of her sandwiches were tuna mayonnaise or cheese sandwiches. She sold 11 fewer cheese sandwiches than she did tuna mayonnaise, so she sold 41 tuna.

7. 1234
R=1, A=2, N=3, G=4

8. 4516
G=4, E=5, R=1, M=6

9. GRAM
G=4, R=1, A=2, M=6

10. 64
Double the numbers each time.

11. 64
The number subtracted decreases by 1 each time: −5, −4, −3, −2, −1.

12. 35
There are two sequences which alternate. In the first sequence, add 3 each time. In the second sequence, add 4 each time.

13. 42
There are two sequences which alternate. In the first sequence, add 5 each time. In the second sequence, add 3 each time.

14. 12
There are two sequences which alternate. In the first sequence, subtract 4 each time. In the second sequence, halve the numbers each time.

Test 28 — pages 73-75

1. 4
Multiply the two outside numbers together.

2. 9
Divide the first number by the third number, then add 3.

3. 14
Add the two outside numbers together, then multiply by 2.

4. 6
Subtract the third number from the first number, then subtract 1.

5. UM
The first letter in the pair moves back 1 letter. The second letter in the pair moves forward 1 letter.

6. XP
The first letter in the pair moves forward 5 letters. The second letter in the pair moves back 8 letters.

7. VD
The first letter in the pair moves back 4 letters. The second letter in the pair moves back 2 letters.

8. HK
The first letter in the pair moves forward 7 letters. The second letter in the pair moves back 2 letters.

9. 16
12 + 14 = 26, 26 = 42 − 16

10. 11
64 ÷ 8 + 6 = 14, 14 = 3 + 11

11. 6
50 ÷ 5 + 2 = 12, 12 = 2 × 6

12. 2
63 ÷ 9 + 2 = 9, 9 = 4 × 2 + 1

13. D
Rory has 1 scoop of chocolate and 1 scoop of strawberry. We are told that he has 1 scoop of strawberry. 3 people have a scoop of chocolate. We know Flavia and Damian's scoops, so Rory, Lucas and Ivy have chocolate.

14. A
Sonia cannot have counted more insects than Demi. Demi and Nick counted 30 insects each and Buana counted 15, so they collectively counted 75. That means that Pete and Sonia collectively found 60 insects. As Pete counts the most insects, he must have counted at least 31. This means that Sonia has counted 29 or fewer insects, which is fewer than Demi, who counted 30.

Test 29 — pages 76-77

1. AF
The first letter in the pair moves forward 4 letters each time. The second letter in the pair moves forward 1 letter each time.

2. HI
The first letter in the pair moves in the sequence +2, +4, +6, +8, +10. The second letter in the pair moves back 2 letters each time.

3. HQ
The first letter in the pair moves back 2 letters each time. The second letter in the pair moves forward 4 letters each time.

4. GF
The first letter in the pair moves in the sequence +1, +3, +5, +7, +9. The second letter in the pair moves in the sequence +2, +3, +4, +5, +6.

5. FH
The first letter in the pair moves forward 4 letters each time. The second letter in the pair moves in the sequence -1, 0, +1, +2, +3.

6. B
26 − 17 = 9, B = 9

7. A
21 ÷ 7 − 2 = 1, A = 1

8. B
15 ÷ 3 − 3 = 2, B = 2

9. D
3 × 2 + 7 − 6 = 7, D = 7

10. 4152
W=4, A=1, R=5, T=2

11. 4532
W=4, R=5, I=3, T=2

12. RAIL
R=5, A=1, I=3, L=6

13. EHRG
To get from the word to the code, move the letters back 1 letter.

14. MOCM
To get from the word to the code, move the letters in the sequence -2, -1, -2, -1.

15. TREK
This is a mirror code, where the letters are an equal distance from the centre of the alphabet. G is a mirror of T, I is a mirror of R, V is a mirror of E and P is a mirror of K.

16. NEWT
To get from the code to the word, move the letters in the sequence -1, -2, -3, -4.

Test 30 — pages 78-79

1. 5
Add the two outside numbers together.

2. 5
Divide the first number by the third number, then add 2.

3. 4
Multiply the two outside numbers together, then divide by 3.

4. 12
Subtract the third number from the first number, then multiply by 3.

5. RP
The first letter in the pair moves back 2 letters. The second letter in the pair moves forward 6 letters.

6. IL
The first letter in the pair moves forward 2 letters. The second letter in the pair moves back 1 letter.

7. OY
The first letter in the pair moves forward 4 letters. The second letter in the pair moves forward 2 letters.

8. SV
ZP and AK are mirror pairs, where the two letters are an equal distance from the centre of the alphabet. The answer will be the mirror pairs for H and E, which are S and V.

9. 5
$54 \div 9 = 6, 6 = 11 - 5$

10. 6
$44 \div 4 + 8 = 19, 19 = 13 + 6$

11. 5
$36 \div 9 + 11 = 15, 15 = 3 \times 5$

12. 4
$72 \div 8 + 2 = 11, 11 = 32 \div 4 + 3$

13. KF
The first letter in the pair moves back 2 letters. The second letter in the pair moves forward 3 letters each time.

14. RN
The first letter in the pair moves in the sequence +1, +3, +5, +7, +9. The second letter in the pair moves back 1 letter each time.

15. PY
The first letter in the pair moves in the sequence +2, +1, 0, −1, −2. The second letter in the pair moves in the sequence +1, +2, +3, +4, +5.

16. CS
The first letter in the pair moves in the sequence +1, +3, +5, +7, +9. The second letter in the pair moves in the sequence +1, -4, +1, -4, +1.

Puzzles 8 — page 80

Dot-to-Dot

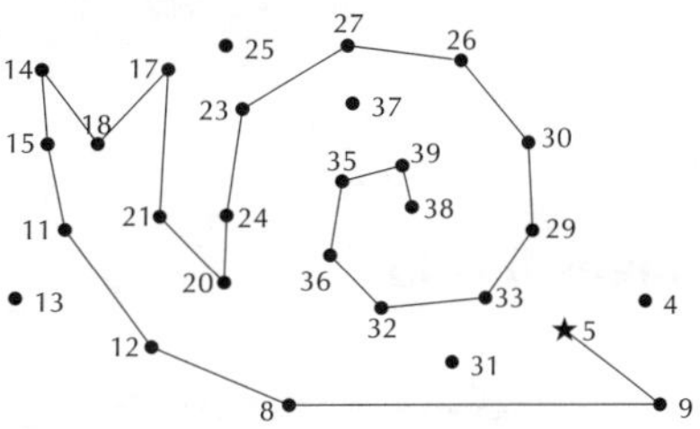

Strange Sums

15 [÷] 3 = 25 [÷] 5 — (5)

11 [−] 3 = 6 [+] 2 — (8)

4 [+] 5 = 27 [÷] 3 — (9)

24 [÷] 4 = 2 [×] 3 — (6)

Test 31 — pages 81-82

1. 12
Subtract 6 each time.

2. 99
The numbers follow the sequence −1, 0, +1, +2, +3.

3. 28
There are two sequences which alternate. In the first sequence, subtract 1. In the second sequence, subtract 5.

4. 4
There are two sequences which alternate. In the first sequence, halve the numbers. In the second sequence, subtract 1.

5. 1
Divide by 3 each time.

6. 4213
O=4, N=2, C=1, E=3

7. 5364
D=5, E=3, M=6, O=4

8. CODE
C=1, O=4, D=5, E=3

9. E
$4 \times 7 = 28, E = 28$

10. E
$4 + 8 - 1 = 11, E = 11$

11. A
$2 \times 9 - 16 = 2, A = 2$

12. C
$2 \times 10 + 1 - 11 = 10, C = 10$

13. SDAJ
To get from the word to the code, move the letters back 4 letters.

14. CITY
To get from the code to the word, move the letters in the sequence +3, −1, +3, −1.

15. SVIW
This is a mirror code, where the letters are an equal distance from the centre of the alphabet. H is a mirror of S, E is a mirror of V, R is a mirror of I and D is a mirror of W.

16. RDMQV
To get from the word to the code, move the letters in the sequence −2, −1, 0, +1, +2.

Test 32 — pages 83-85

1. PU
The first letter in the pair moves forward 2 letters. The second letter in the pair moves forward 1 letter each time.

2. DI
The first letter in the pair moves in the sequence +1, +3, +5, +7, +9. The second letter in the pair moves forward 3 letters each time.

3. II
The first letter in the pair moves in the sequence +5, +4, +3, +2, +1. The second letter in the pair moves in the sequence +2, +3, +2, +3, +2.

4. XE
The first letter in the pair moves in the sequence +1, +3, +5, +7, +9. The second letter in the pair moves in the sequence -2, -5, -2, -5, -2.

5. C
Sanjiv has at least 2 lives left. Camilla has more than 2 lives left, so she must have 3,4 or 5 lives. Sanjiv has 1 fewer life than Camilla, so he must have 2, 3 or 4 lives.

6. B
Betsy goes on one ride. Akan goes on one more ride than her. Akan goes on the dodgems and the waltzers. He doesn't go on any other rides, because he goes on fewer than Jaya, who goes on three. Jaya goes on the most rides. We know that she goes on the dodgems, so she must also go on the roller coaster and the big wheel, as Valter and Akan both go on two rides.

7. ML
The first letter in the pair moves back 8 letters. The second letter in the pair moves forward 5 letters.

8. PJ
The first letter in the pair moves forward 6 letters. The second letter in the pair moves back 6 letters.

9. TK
The first letter in the pair moves back 6 letters. The second letter in the pair moves back 2 letters.

10. FD
GJ and TQ are mirror pairs, where the two letters are an equal distance from the centre of the alphabet. The answer will be the mirror pairs for U and W, which are F and D.

11. 17
$36 \div 9 = 4, 4 = 21 - 17$

12. 6
$25 \div 5 + 13 = 18, 18 = 3 \times 6$

13. 3
$18 \div 9 + 10 = 12, 12 = 36 \div 3$

14. 5
$24 \div 3 + 12 = 20, 20 = 100 \div 5$

Test 33 — pages 86-87

1. 42
Multiply the two outside numbers together, then subtract 3.

2. 10
Multiply the two outside numbers together, then divide by 3.

3. 2
Divide the first number by the third number, then subtract 2.

4. 20
Subtract the third number from the first number, then multiply by the first number.

5. 6124
S=6, K=1, I=2, N=4

6. 3546
P=3, A=5, N=4, S=6

7. SPIN
S=6, P=3, I=2, N=4

8. E
$9 \times 3 = 27, E = 27$

9. A
$21 \div 7 - 2 = 1, A = 1$

10. E
$3 \times 5 - 6 = 9, E = 9$

11. B
$7 \times 3 - 14 = 7, B = 7$

12. C
$2 \times 3 + 12 - 10 = 8, C = 8$

13. VH
The first letter in the pair moves forward 3 letters. The second letter in the pair moves back 8 letters.

14. GW
The first letter in the pair moves back 4 letters. The second letter in the pair moves forward 5 letters.

15. IT
The first letter in the pair moves forward 4 letters. The second letter in the pair moves forward 1 letter.

16. KK
The first letter in the pair moves forward 1 letter. The second letter in the pair moves back 6 letters.

Test 34 — pages 88-90

1. HKPF
To get from the word to the code, move the letters forwards 2 letters.

2. DYYJ
To get from the word to the code, move the letters in the sequence +2, -2, +2, -2.

3. PAST
To get from the code to the word, move the letters in the sequence +1, 0, -1, -2.

4. TILT
To get from the code to the word, move the letters in the sequence -2, -4, -6, -8.

5. 5
There are two sequences which alternate. In the first sequence, halve the numbers each time. In the second sequence, subtract 1 each time.

6. 14
The number subtracted increases by 1 each time: −5, −6, −7, −8, −9.

7. 40
The number subtracted increases by 2 each time: −1, −3, −5, −7, −9.

8. 37
There are two sequences which alternate. In the first sequence, subtract 3 each time. In the second sequence, subtract 2 each time.

9. 100
Multiply the first number by the third number, then multiply the answer by the third number.

10. 4
Subtract the third number from the first number, then subtract 2.

11. 5
Subtract the third number from the first number, then add 3.

12. 7
Add the two outside numbers together, then add the first number.

13. B
The second lightest pig weighs less than 13kg. The lightest pig is three times lighter than the heaviest, so it weighs 8kg. All 5 pigs weigh between 70 and 75kg, which means the 2 unknown pigs must weigh between 20 and 25kg in total. The second lightest pig must weigh at least 9kg. The third heaviest pig weighs an odd number of kilograms, so it could weigh 15, 13 or 11kg. The second lightest pig could weigh 9, 10, 11 or 12kg.

14. C
Steph gets less pocket money than Zahir. Sam gets the least pocket money, so he must get less than £10, which Amala receives. The maximum amount Sam can get is £9.99. Steph gets 3 times as much as Sam, so her maximum amount is £29.97.

Puzzles 9 — page 91

Pearly Problems
The thief is **Lady Lucinda**. She is the only person who is not doing anything between 3-4pm. Prince Percy goes for a walk with Lady Lucinda from 2-3pm. Lady Lucinda goes shopping for hats an hour after getting back from her walk, so from 4pm. She does not say that she is doing anything between 3-4pm.

Test 35 — pages 92-94

1. 15
Subtract 4 each time.

2. 47
The number subtracted increases by 2 each time: −1, −3, −5, −7, −9.

3. 30
There are two sequences which alternate. In the first sequence, add 2 each time. In the second sequence, subtract 3 each time.

4. 22
The number added moves in the sequence +1, +1, +2, +3, +5, +8, where the two previous increments are added together.

5. 2
There are two sequences which alternate. In the first sequence, the number subtracted is halved each time: −8, −4, −2. In the second sequence, the number added is doubled each time: +5, +10.

6. A
Jemima baked the most biscuits. Anwar baked the second highest number of biscuits. Elsie and Theresa both baked half the number of biscuits that Anwar did. Bob baked the fewest. Jemima must have baked the most, because everyone else baked fewer biscuits than she did.

7. C
Greta cannot have coffee. More people have tea than coffee. We know that Gautam has coffee and Anna has tea. Greta and Lisa have the same drink, so they must have tea. If they had coffee, then more people would have coffee than tea.

8. 11
Divide the first number by the third number, then add 4.

9. 18
Multiply the two outside numbers together, then divide by 2.

10. 16
Add together the two outside numbers, then add 3.

11. 4
Divide the first number by the third number, then add the third number.

12. 1356
S=1, A=3, L=5, T=6

13. 4216
R=4, E=2, S=1, T=6

14. STAR
S=1, T=6, A=3, R=4

Test 36 — pages 95-97

1. LW
The first letter in the pair moves back 1 letter each time. The second letter in the pair moves back 5 letters each time.

2. FQ
The first letter in the pair moves in the sequence +1, +3, +5, +7, +9. The second letter in the pair moves forward 2 letters each time.

3. MY
The first letter in the pair moves in the sequence +4, −1, +4, −1, +4. The second letter in the pair moves in the sequence −1, −2, −3, −4, −5.

4. SH
The first letter in the pair moves in the sequence −5, +3, −5, +3, −5. The second letter in the pair moves in the sequence +2, +4, +6, +8, +10.

5. E
$4 + 12 - 1 = 15$, E = 15

6. D
$60 \div 5 + 3 = 15$, D = 15

7. E
$6 \times 3 + 6 = 24$, E = 24

8. D
$18 \div 6 \times 5 + 1 = 16$, D = 16

9. C
$3 \times 4 + 2 - 10 = 4$, C = 4

10. 2346
R=2, O=3, T=4, E=6

11. 5614
K=5, E=6, P=1, T=4

12. PORK
P=1, O=3, R=2, K=5

13. D
One of the caterpillars eats 19 leaves. Only 1 caterpillar eats less than 20 leaves. If 1 caterpillar ate 19 leaves, the caterpillar that ate the most must eat 38 leaves. Only 2 of the caterpillars eat more than 25 leaves each, but only 1 eats less than 20. The total number of leaves is 100, therefore none of the caterpillars must eat 19 leaves.

14. C
Mohammed catches a train after 4 pm. The direct train takes 3 hours 45 minutes. The earliest direct train he could catch would be at 5 pm because he would arrive in Hancaster at 8:45 pm. The earliest train Mohammed could catch that stops in Garrington is at 4:30 pm, because it arrives at 8:40 pm.

Test 37 — pages 98-99

1. 4
$16 + 27 = 43$, $43 = 47 - 4$

2. 8
$18 \div 2 + 7 = 16$, $16 = 2 \times 8$

3. 5
$28 \div 4 + 6 = 13$, $13 = 3 \times 6 - 5$

4. 5
$9 \times 2 - 1 = 17$, $17 = 14 + 5 - 2$

5. BO
The first letter in the pair moves back 4 letters.
The second letter in the pair moves forward 5 letters.

6. CF
The first letter in the pair moves back 3 letters.
The second letter in the pair moves back 5 letters.

7. HY
The first letter in the pair moves back 2 letters.
The second letter in the pair moves forward 2 letters.

8. PF
AZ and ZA are mirror pairs, where the two letters are an equal distance from the centre of the alphabet. The answer will be the mirror pairs for K and U, which are P and F.

9. SELL
To get from the code to the word, move the letters in the sequence +1, -2, +1, -2.

10. OAGP
To get from the word to the code, move the letters in the sequence +2, -4, +2, -4.

11. LMQD
To get from the word to the code, move the letters in the sequence -1, -2, -3, -4.

12. DINT
This is a mirror code, where the letters are an equal distance from the centre of the alphabet. W is a mirror of D, R is a mirror of I, M is a mirror of N and G is a mirror of T.

13. 40
Add 4 each time.

14. 49
The numbers follow the sequence −2, −1, 0, +1, +2.

15. 2
There are two sequences which alternate. In the first sequence, subtract 4 each time. In the second sequence, add 3 each time.

16. 32
There are two sequences which alternate. In the first sequence, add 6 each time. In the second sequence, halve the numbers each time.

Puzzles 10 — page 100

Minnie Moaner's Wordoku

N	A	C	M	P	L	T	O	I
O	M	P	A	T	I	N	L	C
I	L	T	O	C	N	M	P	A
A	T	L	N	O	M	C	I	P
M	C	N	L	I	P	A	T	O
P	I	O	T	A	C	L	M	N
L	P	I	C	N	T	O	A	M
T	N	A	I	M	O	P	C	L
C	O	M	P	L	A	I	N	T

The word spelt is complaint.

Treehouse Tricks
Serena's nickname is Ueveta.
Charlotte's nickname is Elaxtodfe.
To create your nickname, the vowels in your name stay the same, and the consonants move in the sequence +2, +4, +6, etc.

Each question uses a different code. Use the alphabet to help you work out the answer to each question.

A B C D E F G H I J K L M N O P Q R S T U V W X Y Z

Example: If the code for **MANY** is **LZMX**, what is the code for **GREY**? (FQDX)

9. If the code for **BURY** is **AWQA**, what is **RGKN** the code for? (____________)

10. If the code for **COAT** is **EKCP**, what is the code for **MEET**? (____________)

11. If the code for **GRID** is **FPFZ**, what is the code for **MOTH**? (____________)

12. If the code for **PATH** is **KZGS**, what is **WRMG** the code for? (____________)

Find the number that continues each sequence in the best way. Write your answer on the line.

Example: 3 6 9 12 15 (18)

13. 20 24 28 32 36 (______)

14. 49 47 46 46 47 (______)

15. 14 28 10 31 6 34 (______)

16. 14 20 20 10 26 5 (______)

END OF TEST

/ 16

Puzzles 10

There's one more to go! This final puzzle page tests your **logic** skills one last time.

Minnie Moaner's Wordoku

Minnie Moaner hates word puzzles, but she always does the one on the back of Whinger's Weekly magazine. Help her out and find the word in the wordoku puzzle.

Complete the grid so that every row, column and 3x3 grid contains nine different letters.

You can only use the letters which are already on the grid.

	A		M				O	I
	M	P	A	T	I	N		
I		T	O				P	
	T	L		O	M	C		
		N				A		O
P	I			A	C		M	
L				N	T		A	
T			I				C	L
	O	M	P	L		I		

What word is spelt in the highlighted row? ____________________

Treehouse Tricks

Members of the top secret treehouse club all must have a secret nickname. These are always related to their names in some way.

A B C D E F G H I J K L M N O P Q R S T U V W X Y Z

Joshua's nickname is Lownua.

Ravi's nickname is Tazi.

Serena's nickname is _ _ _ _ _ _.

Charlotte's nickname is _ _ _ _ _ _ _ _ _.

What's your nickname? ____________________

VLXPE1